Great Issues of the Day

Number Three

ISSN 0270-7497

I0142032

FIDEL BY FIDEL

An Interview with Dr. Fidel Castro Ruz
President of the Republic of Cuba

Conducted by

Jeffrey M. Elliot

& Mervyn M. Dymally

R. REGINALD
The Borgo Press
San Bernardino, California □ MCMXCVI

THE BORGO PRESS

Publishers of Fine Books Since 1975
Post Office Box 2845
San Bernardino, CA 92406
United States of America

*   *   *   *   *   *   *

Library of Congress Cataloging-in-Publication Data

Castro, Fidel, 1927-
  [Nada podra detener la marcha de la historia. English]
  Fidel by Fidel : an interview with Dr. Fidel Castro Ruz, President of the
Republic of Cuba / conducted by Jeffrey M. Elliot and Mervyn M. Dymally.
    p. cm. — (Great issues of the day, ISSN 0270-7497 ; no. 3)
  Selections from an interview given by Fidel Castro to Jeffrey M. Elliot
and Mervyn M. Dymally in Mar. 1985, and published in full under title: Nada
podra detener la marcha de la historia.
  Includes index.
  ISBN 0-89370-330-3 (cloth). — ISBN 0-89370-430-X (paper)
  1. Castro, Fidel, 1927- —Interviews. 2. Cuba—Politics and government—
1959- . 3. Latin America—Politics and government—1948- . 4. World
politics—1945- . 5. Heads of state—Cuba—Interviews. I. Elliot, Jeffrey M.
II. Dymally, Mervyn M., 1926- . III. Title. IV. Series.
F1788.22.C3A25 1996   85-25551
972.91'064—dc19   CIP

FIRST EDITION

CONTENTS

DEDICATION

For Dr. Rolin G. Mainuddin

A superb scholar, an inspiring teacher,
and a steadfast friend

INTRODUCTION

During an extraordinary nine-day visit to Havana, Cuba, on March 22-30, 1985, Dr. Jeffrey M. Elliot, Professor of Political Science at North Carolina Central University, and Rep. Mervyn M. Dymally (D-Calif.), Ph.D., Member of the House Committee on Foreign Affairs, and Founding President of the Caribbean-American Research Institute, conducted a series of illuminating interviews with Fidel Castro. Each night at approximately eleven P.M., a limosine would arrive at their hotel and take them to the Presidential Palace, where they would talk candidly with the President until dawn. When they left Havana, they took with them twenty-five hours of tapes, undoubtedly the most wide-ranging and candid discussions ever conducted with Castro. Published here for the first time are this controversial and flamboyant leader's opinions on American foreign policy, U.S.-Cuban relations, the New International Economic Order, unity and disunity in Latin America, political revolution, right-wing dictatorships, the evils of capitalism, the arms race, Reagan's economic policies, the effects of the economic blockade on Cuba, and the need for peaceful coexistence between the superpowers. Also included are many personal insights into Castro himself—his character, his revolution, his people, his Cuba.

Fidel Castro Ruz was born in Birán, in the former province of Oriente, on August 13, 1926, the scion of a wealthy land-owner family. He received his primary education in a rural school and later attended private boarding schools in Santiago de Cuba and Havana. In September, 1945, he entered the School of Law at the University of Havana, where he received his Ph.D. in law and an additional degree in international law.

While at the university, he founded and led numerous student committees, participating in various demonstrations and movements directed against the administration then in power. More than once he was beaten, wounded, or imprisoned. In 1947, he joined the expedition that attempted to overthrow the Trujillo dictatorship in Santo Domingo. As a student leader, Castro traveled to Venezuela, Panamá, and Colombia to organize a Latin American "anti-imperialist" student congress. While in Bogotá, he supported the popular uprising of April, 1948. During his student years, he also participated in the political movement that gave rise to the Cuban People's Party. An active participant in the

5

student wing, he sought to organize a mass movement of a revolutionary nature.

After President Fulgencio Batista's *coup d'état* of March 10, 1952, Castro concentrated on recruiting soldiers for what he believed would be an inevitable armed struggle against the self-proclaimed president. He organized and led an attack against the "Moncada" barracks on July 26, 1953. He was captured and then imprisoned. During his trial he first articulated many of his revolutionary ideas, including his famous remark: "History will absolve me." He was sentenced to fifteen years servitude on the infamous Isle of Pines. However, as a result of intense public clamor, he was released on May 15, 1955.

After leaving prison, Castro founded the July 26 Movement. On July 7, he left for México, and later visited the United States, where he attempted to raise funds for an armed invasion of Cuba. On December 2, 1956, Castro approached the Cuban coast with eighty-two men aboard the yacht *Granma*. After an initial setback, he was able to reorganize his forces and successfully pursue his struggle in the Sierra Maestra mountains. For two years, he directed the operations of the Rebel Army, personally commanding Column 1, known as the "José Martí" brigade, participating in all of the major operations and battles along the First Front.

On January 1, 1959, upon receiving news of Batista's flight, Castro called for a general strike to consolidate the revolutionary movement. The following day, he was named Commander-in-Chief of all air, sea, and land forces. On February 13, he was selected Prime Minister of the Revolutionary Government, and on May 17, President of the National Institute of Agrarian Reform.

Since then, Castro has consolidated his control of Cuba, and is probably one of the few socialist or communist leaders in the world today who could win a freely-conducted election. His personal popularity in Cuba remains unchallenged. Among the government posts he has held are: First Secretary of the Integrated Revolutionary Organizations, Secretary-General of the Unified Party of the Socialist Revolution of Cuba, First Secretary of the Central Committee of the Communist Party, and President of the Councils of State and of Ministers. He presently serves as President and Commander-in-Chief, and has recently named his younger brother, Raúl, as his future successor, subject to confirmation by the appropriate governmental bodies.

A note on the text: the tapes were originally transcribed by the Cuban government from the Spanish and English originals (Castro, although he understands English, will never speak it in a formal interview), the Spanish portions being translated virtually word-for-word into English. Because Castro tends to speak in long, complicated sentences, reiterating the points he wishes to make with repetitive phrases and by restating his themes, extensive editing was required to produce a much reduced text that nonetheless maintains the essence of what he was trying to say. Parts of the text are very similar to other interviews he gave during this same period (of about three months) to Spanish and Mexican journalists, and to American television broadcasters.

—Boden Clarke
San Bernardino, California
May 1, 1996

A FIDEL CASTRO CHRONOLOGY

1926   Fidel Castro Ruz is born on a farm in the Mayarí municipality in the province of Oriente on August 13 (some sources claim 1927). His father, Angel Castro y Arguz, is a native of Galicia, Spain. A moderately wealthy sugarcane planter, Angel Castro fathers seven children, two by his first wife. While still married to her, he fathers five more children by his cook, Lina Ruz González, a native Cuban. Fidel is the second of these.

1945   Castro enters the School of Law of the University of Havana, from which he receives a doctor of laws degree in 1950.

1947   Joins the expedition (based on Cayo Confites) led by Dominican exiles and Cubans to overthrow General Rafael L. Trujillo of the Dominican Republic. The attempt is quashed by the Cuban government. He becomes a member of the Cuban People's Party (called Ortodoxos).

1948   Participates in riots that erupt during the Ninth International Conference of the American States in Bogotá, Colombia. He marries Mirta Díaz-Bilart, with whom he has one son, Fidel Castro Díaz-Balart.

1952   Fidel Castro becomes the Ortodoxos candidate for a seat in the House of Representatives (from a district in Havana) in the elections scheduled for 1952. In March, 1952, however, former Cuban president, General Fulgencio Batista y Zaldívar, overthrows the government of President Carlos Prío Socarrás in a military coup and cancels the elections.

1953   Castro leads a small band of 165 rebels in a failed attack on the Moncada Cuban army barracks in Santiago de Cuba; about 100 students and soldiers are killed. He escapes but is soon arrested, convicted, and sentenced to 15 years' imprisonment. The Bishop of Santiago and other civic leaders pressure the regime to spare the lives of those who have been captured. A subsequently edited version of Castro's self-defense at his trial is heralded as his major statement during the 1950s. Known by its concluding words, "History Will Absolve Me" (La Historia Me Absolvera), it attacks the anticonstitutional, repressive, and corrupt practices of the Batista government, calling for political and civil liberties. It also calls for a land reform and other rural improvement programs, along with programs for industrialization, the partial sharing of profits between shareholders and workers, and a pledge not to introduce new taxes. At the time, his political ideas are nationalist, antiimperialist, and reformist; he is *not* a member of the Communist party.

1954 Released in a general amnesty and goes into exile in México. His rebel group becomes known as the "26 July Movement."

1955 Fidel Castro and his wife, Mirta Díaz-Bilart Castro, divorce.

1956 Castro leaves México with 86 followers, including Ernesto "Che" Guevara, aboard a small sailing vessel, the *Granma*. He lands in Cuba, and although pursued by the military, manages to escape with a dozen survivors into the Sierra Maestra mountains of southwestern Oriente province where he establishes his rebel base. Castro's forces wage guerrilla warfare against the demoralized, ill-equipped, and badly led armed forces of Batista.

1957 About 100 rebels storm Batista's palace. José Antonio Echevarría, President of the Federation of University Students (University of Havana) is killed in a shootout with the police. A mutiny takes place at the Cienfuegos Naval Base. The city of Cienfuegos falls to the rebels. Batista uses bombers, tanks, and armored cars in the fight and several hundred rebels are killed. Lieutenant San Román, leader of the rebels, is captured. He is tortured for months, only to be killed without a trial.

1958 The United States suspends all arms shipments to Batista. A general strike is called by the 26 July Movement, and the civic resistance fails. Elections are held. Batista claims victory for his candidates.

1959 Batista is driven into exile by Castro's forces, paving the way for the latter's rise to power. The 26 July Movement takes over virtual control of the government, and Castro marches into Havana. The leader of the revolutionary forces, he forms a new government. Lléo Manuel Urrutia, a former judge, is proclaimed president of the new regime. Castro himself assumes the premiership on February 16; he relinquishes that post briefly in July in order to force the ouster of the more moderate Urrutia. Promising to establish an honest government, restore the 1940 constitution, guarantee a free press, and respect individual rights and private property, Castro wins the support of the majority of the Cuban people. He attacks the United States and campaigns against "Yankee imperialism" in an effort to become the leader of the Latin American left. His government confiscates more than $1 billion of American-owned property in Cuba, severs trade with the United States, imprisons and executes Americans, and forces most of them to leave the island. At the same time, the Castro government takes over Cuban industry and commerce and allies Cuba with the Communist bloc. It executes more than 1,000 former members of the Batista regime and Castro's own followers who oppose his policy of leading Cuba into the Communist orbit. It seizes all private schools and begins the Communist indoctrination of youth.

1960   Cuba and the USSR sign a sugar agreement. The United States cuts financial aid to Cuba. Virtual censorship is imposed in Cuba. The United States and Great Britain reject Cuban demands that their companies in Cuba refine Soviet crude oil. The U.S. slashes the Cuban sugar quota by 95%. Havana nationalizes all remaining American properties. Soviet Premier Nikita Khrushchev threatens Soviet retaliation if the U.S. intervenes militarily against Cuba. Cuba receives its first Soviet military aid.

1961   The United States breaks off diplomatic relations with Cuba on January 3. Castro declares that "I have been a Marxist-Leninist all along, and will remain one until I die." Cuba aligns itself with the Soviet Union, which grants it massive economic, technical, and military assistance until 1991. The U.S. government equips thousands of Cuban exiles to overthrow Castro's government; their landing at the Bay of Pigs in April, however, fails. He is awarded the Lenin Peace Prize (USSR).

1962   The Soviet Union stations ballistic missiles in Cuba, and the world comes close to nuclear war. The crisis ends when the Soviet Union agrees to withdraw its nuclear weapons from Cuba in exchange for a pledge that the U.S. will not seek to overthrow the Cuban government. Nevertheless, the U.S. Central Intelligence Agency continues to plot Castro's assassination. The Cuban missile crisis dramatizes the Cuban-Soviet alliance.

1963 Castro is awarded the hero of the Soviet Union Award (USSR).

1964 All members of the Organization of American States (OAS), with the exception of México, vote unanimously to break diplomatic and economic links with Cuba.

1965 More than one-quarter million Cubans arrive in the United States through the Freedom Flights program, which is terminated in August, 1971.

1966 A tricontinental conference is held in Havana. Soviet-Cuban tensions reach a high point.

1967 Ernesto "Che" Guevara, the Argentine born Cuban revolutionary leader and architect of the Cuban policy of exporting guerrilla warfare, is slain while trying to foment revolution in Bolivia. Twenty-seven Latin American delegations assemble in Havana and the Latin American Solidarity Organization is established. It includes representatives from all the Latin American countries, as well as Puerto Rico and Trinidad-Tobago.

1967 Puerto Rican "freedom fighters" set up a "Free Puerto Rico Embassy" in Havana.

1968 Castro supports the Soviet invasion of Czechoslovakia, inaugurating a new phase in Cuban-Soviet relations.

1969 The Cuban government mobilizes the nation for a sugar harvest of 10 million tons, the largest in its history.

1970 Castro acknowledges Cuba's failure to meet its 10 million-ton sugar harvest target. The Soviet KGB consolidates its takeover of the Direccion General de Inteligencia (DGI), Cuba's intelligence organization.

1972 Cuba is admitted to the Council for Mutual Economic Assistance (COMECON), the Communist bloc trade association. Castro is awarded the Order of Lenin (Soviet Union).

1973 Cuba sends 500 tank drivers to fight for Syria in the Yom Kippur War with Israel.

1975 The OAS lifts its trade embargo against Cuba. Castro sends troops to support the Soviet-backed Marxist Popular Movement for the Liberation of Angola. At its peak, nearly 32,000 Cuban troops are stationed in Angola with additional troops in

Ethiopia, South Yemen, and elsewhere. The first Cuban Communist Party Congress commences. It announces the first Cuban Five-Year Plan and the ratification of the new socialist constitution.

1976 Castro becomes the head of state and president of the Council of State and Council of Ministers. He also receives the Order of the October Revolution from the Soviet Union.

1977 He tours black Africa and visits Moscow. The U.S. lifts the ban on travel to Cuba. The Carter administration challenges the Cuban presence in Zaire. The tentative normalization of U.S.-Cuban relations begins with the opening of interest sections. A U.S. interest section in Havana is housed in the Swiss embassy and a Cuban interest section in Washington is housed in the Czechoslovakian embassy. The U.S. expresses concern over the presence of 27,000 Cuban troops in Africa. Cuban troops, armed and supplied by the Soviet Union, assist Ethiopia in defeating an invasion by Somalia.

1978 Cuban troops become involved in the invasion of Zaire's Shaba Province by Katangan rebels.

1979 The Frente Sandinista de Libracion Nacional, with Cuban political, economic, logistical, and military assistance, overthrows the government of President Anastasio Somoza in Nicaragua. The Non-Aligned Movement convenes in Havana and Castro is elected chairman. He launches a vast reorganization of the government. Thousands of Cuban "undesirables" are allowed to leave the country in a mass exodus. He continues to insist that normalization of relations with the United States could be negotiated if the U.S. were to end its economic embargo.

1980 Ten thousand Cubans storm the grounds of the Peruvian embassy in Havana seeking political asylum. Taking advantage of a temporary relaxation of emigration restrictions, an additional 120,000 Cubans aboard small boats make the exodus from the port of Mariel in Cuba to the United States. U.S. President Jimmy Carter states that the presence of a Soviet Brigade in Cuba is not acceptable.

1981 The failure of the final guerrilla offensive in El Salvador embarrasses the Cubans who backed the guerrillas and predicted a Nicaragua-like victory. As a result of the escalation of Cuban support for guerrilla movements in Latin America, Cuban relations deteriorate with Ecuador, Colombia, Costa Rica, and

Jamaica, all of which either break relations or withdraw their ambassadors. Cuba announces a joint-venture law designed to attract foreign capital.

1982 Castro reports 120,000 Cuban servicemen abroad, with an additional 30,000 doctors, teachers, engineers, and technicians, including 2,000 military advisers in Nicaragua. Four high-ranking Cuban government officials are indicted by a U.S. Federal grand jury on charges of smuggling narcotics into the United States.

1983 Castro declares a state of "National Alert" in August. Cuban forces are engaged by U.S. marines during their successful invasion of Grenada.

1984 In July negotiations begin with the U.S. on immigration and repatriation; agreement is reached in December.

1985 Cuban undesirables are repatriated to Cuba. Radio Martí is founded by the Voice of America to broadcast news to Cuba, which promptly suspends the immigration agreement.

1986 A number of Cuban political prisoners and their families are allowed to immigrate to the U.S. One-third of the Politburo is replaced at the Third Congress of the Cuban Communist Party.

1987 The 1984 repatriation accord is restored, resulting in riots in U.S. prisons among the Cuban prisoners to be returned to Cuba. Cuba continues to release political prisoners during the next several years.

1988 Cuba's foreign debt per capita has now become one of the largest in the third world.

1989 A number of senior Cuban military officers are implicated in drug smuggling to Columbia and the U.S. General Arnaldo Ochoa Sánchez, Angolan war hero, is tried and executed for treason, and other officers and ministers are tried and/or purged. Withdrawal of Cuban troops from Angola begins. President Gorbachev of the Soviet Union visits Cuba. Castro later attacks the Soviet leader's reform ideas.

1990 TV Martí, sister station of Radio Martí, begins broadcasting to Cuba. Castro announces plans to cut the Communist Party bureaucracy by half. Rationing is extended in November to all products.

1991   The last Cuban troops leave Angola. The Soviet Union announces plans to withdraw its military advisers from Cuba. At the Fourth Party Congress, half of the Central Committee is replaced, and other reforms are announced, including the right of Christians to now join the Party.

1992   Several Cuban dissidents are arrested and executed. The U.S. imposes further economic sanctions on Cuba, adopting the Cuban Democracy Act, which forbids foreign subsidiaries of American companies to deal with Cuba. The construction of Cuba's sole nuclear power station is suspended for lack of money.

1993   The last Russian troops leave Cuba. The ban on Cubans owning foreign currency is lifted.

1994   The Cuban government takes steps to respond to its deteriorating economy and budget deficit, including imposition of an income tax and a reduction of state subsidies. Cubans riot in Havana. An agreement is reached to allow Cubans to immigrate to the U.S.

1995   The U.N. General Assembly adopts a resolution demanding that the U.S. repeal its economic embargo against Cuba.

1996   Two unarmed planes operated by Brothers to the Rescue, a Miami-based Cuban exiles organization, are shot down in international waters by Cuban jets. The U.S. tightens economic sanctions against Cuba, aimed at curbing foreign investment in the Cuban economy.

I.

THE ECONOMIC CRISIS IN LATIN AMERICA AND THE THIRD WORLD

ELLIOT: Mr. President, given the importance of the economic crisis which currently grips Latin America and the Third World, why haven't the industrialized nations responded with greater urgency?

CASTRO: There are several reasons. First, because of their indifference to, and lack of any real concern for, the economic, social, and human tragedy which the Third World countries are currently experiencing. Secondly, due to their collective irresponsibility and lack of foresight concerning the serious political problems which exist in Latin America, particularly in the short and medium term. It's quite possible that when Latin America's economic problems finally reach a crisis stage—and such a crisis is inevitable—the western countries will finally demonstrate some belatedly selfish concern, mainly due to the impact on their own economies. By then, of course, it will be too late. Thirdly, because of their inherent selfishness. You in the West enjoy a privileged economic relationship with the Third World: you buy cheap raw materials from poorer countries, for which you pay less and less, and then sell back to us ever-more-expensive "refined" products which we can't really afford. Finally, because they have become accustomed to a system of interacting economic and social privileges which they find both comfortable and comforting, and which they cannot and will not renounce voluntarily.

In 1984, for example, Latin America transferred more than $70 billion in goods to the industrialized countries. This includes interest on foreign debts, overseas profits of $37.3 billion, and a $20 billion trade deficit between Latin America and the rest of the world. What does this mean in real terms? If Latin America had been able to purchase with its exports the equivalent of 100 products from the industrialized world in 1980, by 1984 it could only acquire 78.3 products, using the same number of exports. The difference amounts to slightly over $20 billion. In effect, during 1984 Latin

America gave away merchandise worth $20 billion or more without receiving anything of value in return.

To these figures we must add—and this is a very conservative estimate—approximately $10 billion in foreign currency sent overseas (mainly to the United States) for reinvestment. Another $5 billion dollars were lost due to the overvaluation of the dollar.

To assess these losses more fully, let us use gold as an example. Imagine that you borrow a kilogram of gold at 6% interest. Historically, interest rates have never been very high under ordinary circumstances; indeed, some countries and religions, particularly Islam and medieval Catholicism, have rejected the charging of interest as a form of institutionalized robbery. But, let's leave aside such considerations, and accept the statement that someone who has borrowed money should repay it with interest. Having borrowing a kilo of gold, you must repay it with 6% interest at the end of the year. Then the lender tells you that interest rates have suddenly risen an additional 35% (a figure more or less equal to the recent overvaluation of the dollar). The single kilo that you borrowed in good faith has suddenly mushroomed to 1.35 kilos due on demand, plus, of course, the original 6% interest. Again for the sake of argument, let's assume that you decide, reluctantly, that you can't afford to offend the lender, and that you agree to pay the new sum. Suddenly, the lender announces that he has arbitrarily raised interest rates again, by an additional 10%. I don't know of any religious, philosophical, or ethical system that would regard such "highway robbery" as moral. Yet, this is precisely the situation in which Latin America now finds itself.

At least two-thirds of Latin America's debt was contracted with American firms—perhaps $200 billion. Let's assume that that figure represents the actual debt in dollars—quite unlikely, since other credit sources have overused that currency—and that the dollar is overvalued by 10%. You have immediately increased the real debt by $20 billion, plus interest, of course.

If the dollar is overvalued by 30%, one's real debt in dollars has suddenly increased by $60 billion. The sum in dollars doesn't change, you understand, but each dollar has become more expensive relative to the debtor country's currency. Therefore, my own rather conservative estimate is that in 1984 Latin America paid at least $5 billion in interest based solely on an overvalued American dollar.

Thus, Latin America transferred more than $70 billion to you in a single year in the form of money or merchandise for which it didn't receive anything tangible in exchange—other than a great many financial headaches.

How much of this is legitimate? I will accept the theory that "normal" interest must be paid on legally-contracted debts, adopting a western or "Christian" view that, for a given amount of money lent, the lender is entitled to a reasonable—though still high—return on his investment (say, 6-8%). So, what share of the $70 billion now being exacted from Latin America is beyond accepted norms, even in the United States? The differences are these: from deterioration in the terms of trade between Latin America and the West— about $20 billion; from charging interest rates of 12% instead of 8%—also a conservative estimate—$10 billion. It's estimated that each additional assessed point of interest increases the amount that Latin America must pay by $3.5 billion annually. One must also add $10 billion for the flight of capital—money that a country has received for exports, or for services rendered, or even for loans. This is money that the country needs for investments or for development, which has been sent overseas to be reinvested in sounder currencies. Add another $5 billion for the overvaluation of the dollar, and you can see we have a real problem here. In my opinion, an opinion many of the leaders of these countries share, the Latin American world was arbitrarily and illegitimately deprived of least $45 billion in 1984. This is a part of the world where the population doubles every 25 years, one which faces terrible social, educational, housing, health, and employment problems. We can't afford to lose $45 billion, or even $1 billion—we need it here, to invest at home in our own people's futures.

We cannot and will not bear this economic burden any longer—we know it, the West knows it, the people know it. Clearly, a crisis is brewing. If the western countries persist in maintaining this system of legal extortion, and if no solution is found, I believe that a generalized social explosion in Latin America is inevitable. Of course, I'm emphasizing and reiterating these facts precisely to make everyone aware of the problem. I've been told by western reporters and western leaders: "You want to see social upheaval in Latin America!" I reply: "No, I want only to see these problems solved; random social unrest solves nothing and only makes things worse."

We must solve this economic crisis, and solve it soon; and we must struggle for the New International Economic Order, which was nearly unanimously adopted by the United Nations 10 years ago to promote international industrial cooperation, and to protect the economic prospects of the weaker countries in the world. The U.N. proposed to end such arbitrary actions as the growing imbalance in trade terms for goods and services sold by the industrialized West to the Third World; such unjust, even abusive (but very common) financial practices as charging artificially high interest; and the overvaluation of the industrialized countries' currencies. Equally loathsome and selfish are practices like the dumping of highly subsidized products onto Third World markets, and protectionist tariffs and other such measures frequently applied by the European Economic

Community and the United States to cheap goods sold by the Third World to the West, goods which are seen to undercut industries already in place in those countries. For example, the United States has long protected its textile industry by surcharging imported clothing.

Let me cite another example of a protectionist policy which has directly affected many countries in Latin America and the Caribbean. In 1981, the United States imported 5 million tons of sugar, most of it from Third World countries. By 1984, however, sugar imports had dropped to just 2.7 million tons—and are still dropping. Economists say that you will be importing less than 1.7 million tons annually by 1987. Why the change? The United States is encouraging the production of domestic beet sugar and corn syrup by subsidizing American farmers. American taxpayers are paying for these subsidies, of course, and are also paying more for sugar, because its price isn't regulated by the law of supply and demand, the system so loudly championed by capitalist economists. I notice that the so-called "free" market in America is free only when it suits your national policy. All too often, however, you erect just as many artificial barriers with subsidies and price supports as the Europeans do.

What has happened to the countries which used to export sugar to the United States? Their exports of this cash crop have been reduced by half, even two-thirds in some cases. This doesn't even take into account customs duties. The Dominican Republic, Jamaica, Colombia, Perú, Ecuador—these are all supposed to be your allies! I don't even mention Cuba—our quota was taken from us a long time ago, under the pretext that the destruction of our economy through an impenetrable blockade would somehow also destroy the Revolution. It didn't, of course, although many of our ordinary farmers suffered as a result. Now you're taking away the basic economic sustenance of your Latin American allies. Why? They haven't had socialist revolutions or moved away from capitalism. What will they do with their untrained workers? What will they do with their idle plantations and failing industries? Most importantly, what about their debts? How can you reasonably expect these countries to repay usurious interest rates while their economic infrastructures are being eaten away? There are no easy answers here.

The United States is doing the same thing with other products: there are restrictions and quotas for textile imports from Latin America, and similar strictures on steel from Brazil, Argentina, and México—and so on and so forth. All of this contradicts the principles of free enterprise, of course, not to mention the laws of supply and demand, and your much-heralded "free" market. New products emerging from Latin American industries to compete in the world market have even fewer prospects.

The European position is even worse: they subsidize sugar at very high prices and export the surplus. Europe once imported millions of tons of sugar from the Third World; it now demands quotas totalling no more than 5 million tons annually worldwide, essentially to protect its own internal interests. All of these measures drive sugar prices down, because if the United States cuts imports by 5 million tons (*i.e.*, in half), and if Europe becomes a net exporter, the surplus is dumped on the world market, and the supply becomes greater than the demand. Then Japan can buy cheaper sugar, Canada can buy cheaper sugar, and the other rich, industrialized countries can all buy cheaper sugar. It's a very cozy arrangement. Other countries with more limited means have unlimited needs for such basic products, but don't have the necessary cash reserves.

Europe also subsidizes meat—in the past, it was a net importer, but now, of course, it exports. In the European Economic Community, producers are paid $2500 a ton, and the meat is then exported for $800 a ton. So, meat from Argentina, Colombia, Brazil, Costa Rica, Panamá, and other Latin American countries must then sell at a depressed market price of $1150 a ton—and it still isn't competitive. As with sugar, many Third World countries need meat desperately, but they can't afford it. Their own production is insufficient to meet domestic needs, and their exports are depressed by the use of quotas and other such gimmicks. Their main clients, the industrialized nations, are paying increasingly laughable prices—and they have no choice but to accept them.

Feeding a large, growing, hungry population requires technology, fertilizer, pesticides, machinery, and energy, and they can only come from the industrialized world, or from the large fuel exporters, at increasingly inaccessible prices. In addition, we need investment capital, technology, and scientific expertise. None of this is within the reach of the Third World. Latin America can't produce these things from thin air, and it certainly can't buy them. This is the tragedy which I see everytime I visit Central and South America.

The New International Economic Order was proposed by myself and others to seek an end to unjust trade practices by the richer, more industrialized countries of the West. Latin America will never develop economically so long as it continues to receive less for its exports while being charged more for its imports; while its hard currency is being drained away overseas; while its exports are restricted; while it is being subjected to devastatingly unfair forms of economic competition; while the dollar (the international trading currency) is overvalued; and while it is charged arbitrarily high interest rates on the enormous debts that have been imposed on it.

So long as the industrialized countries maintain this system of privileges for themselves, they are acting as modern-day equivalents of our colonial masters of 200 years ago. Clearly, the West is not interested in giving up this system—it does so much for you and so little for us. You certainly would not sit still for one minute if Russia, for example, your sworn enemy in the world, tried to enslave you in a form of economic bondage. Yet this is just what you are doing to us. The Third World, which for centuries have supplied exotic products, raw materials, and cheap fuel to their economic masters, are certainly not the ones to blame for their economic backwardness.

DYMALLY: In which of the Latin American countries is this economic crisis you speak of most severe—and why?

CASTRO: The worst situation is in Bolivia, where the gross national product dropped by 16.1% between 1981 and 1984, and the per capita GNP by a staggering 24.6%. The value of Bolivia's exports dropped from $828 million to $730 million in just two years, from 1982-1984. Its modest imports increased during the same period from $429 million to $460 million—a meager amount by western standards. Yet, it is practically impossible for a country with Bolivia's growing, poverty-stricken population, lack of economic infrastructure, and basic food and fuel requirements, to survive with only $460 million worth of imports. Somehow the Bolivian government managed during this period to build a favorable balance of trade amounting to roughly $270 million annually, all of which had to be used to service the interest on its debts (not even the debt itself!), and contributed nothing directly to Bolivia's economy. How do you tell scores of starving Indians that the money that could have bought foodstuffs, medicines, farm implements, or educational facilities went instead to Bolivia's rich foreign masters? In such economic "basket cases," which I think is the word you westerners like to use, the International Monetary Fund's pitiful attempts to "correct" their economic problems (*i.e.*, making certain western banks are repaid their loans plus exorbitant amounts of interest) has translated into domestic political and social upheavals, ultimately resulting in situations where the local people become totally opposed to the imposition of any new measures which will lower their already abysmal standards of living or which will impose unacceptable personal sacrifices. When a laborer needs bread just to keep his children from starving, he will not willingly accept his government's attempts to take it away from him.

Almost simultaneously, democratic governments have sprung up in three important Latin American countries: Argentina, Uruguay, and Brazil. Uruguay's return to democracy is important not because of its size or resources, but because of its symbolism. After long years of military oppression, Uruguay has finally turned to a constitutional regime. Here is a country that had been a model of democratic institutions for a very long time; like Chile, it was once called the "Switzerland of the Americas."

The Reagan Administration proudly proclaims the fact (almost presenting it as a result of its own policies) that democracy has returned to Latin America, again showing its ignorance of both the past and the present simultaneously. Democracy has never left Latin America, but neither will it remain very long under the present circumstances. What is really moving forward is the steadily increasing economic crisis.

This reestablishment of democratic governments has, of course, occurred for mostly local reasons, including a pervasive dissatisfaction with military rule. Certainly, a contributing factor is the fact that the economic crisis in South America has become so serious that the military, demoralized and bewildered by public outcries and their own evident inability to rule, feel incapable of handling the situation. So they have withdrawn from the scene, one by one, like rats scurrying for their holes. If the economic situation had been less serious, they might have resisted a little longer. Instead, they turned the administration of the state over to civilians, bequeathing them a terrible inheritance.

If the economic problems stemming from the debt aren't resolved, these fragile democratic institutions will inevitably crumble, leaving in their wake utter chaos and a power vacuum. This is a prescription for revolution, my friends—remember you heard it here first.

Experts close to the new government have said that Uruguay's foreign debt now totals $5.5 billion, while exports are just $1 billion annually. Uruguay's economic future does not look good. Important domestic industries, such as textiles, have been severely impacted by recent protectionist measures in the United States. Its meat exports have been affected by quotas imposed by the European Economic Community, whose meat production is subsidized. Consequently, the Uruguayan standard of living dropped by 50% during the years the military government was in power, a fact which directly led to the fall of the military regime there. The democratic government of a country where civilians have recently taken control after years of savage repression cannot possibly apply the International Monetary Fund's stringent economic measures and expect to survive, much less demand new sacrifices of its people. The democratic regimes in Argentina and Brazil face similar quandaries.

The new leaders of these three countries, men and women who kept the democractic flame burning during the long years of dictatorship, will not suddenly order the army or the police into the streets just to keep the IMF happy—give them credit for a little more intelligence than that. The first aim of any government is its survival, and the second, if the governmental leaders are responsible men and women, is to do as much as possible for as many of its citizens as it can. There is no possible way that these leaders will try to extort every last cent of their debts from their unwilling masses, and this is the only way it could be done.

In their public statements and private consultations these presidents and politicians have made three things perfectly clear: that they will not burden their people with the consequences of the debt, that they will not knowingly force their countries into recession or depression, and that they will not sacrifice their nations' industrial development. What hasn't yet been determined is how such statements can be reconciled with the ever-growing problem of the debt.

The International Monetary Fund demands reductions in inflation rates, controls over budgetary deficits, and restrictive measures to increase unemployment and aggravate economic problems that have been accumulating for decades. Consumer prices in Latin America rose by an average of 130.8% percent in 1983, and by 175.4% in 1984. With such inflation heating local economies, management of the debt becomes impossible. The inflation has resulted, of course, from governments trying to maintain a sliding standard of living by printing currency that is not supported by any real economic growth. The cycle quickly begins feeding on itself, unless extremely stringent wage-and-price controls are instituted. And even when controls are imposed, as has already occurred in Brazil and Argentina, maintaining them for any length of time against cries of consumer outrage is almost impossible. In both countries inflation is again creeping upward.

It is increasingly difficult under such circumstances to demand that the Latin American countries—whose economies have not only stagnated in recent years, but actually regressed, while their populations have continued to grow at a high rate—extract $40 billion from their overburdened economies each year, just to pay the interest on their foreign debts. What new sacrifices would these countries have to make, what internal restrictions would they have to apply, in order to drain such fabulous sums from their economies while simultaneously reducing inflation and promoting internal development? They would lose all prospects and hopes for the future. What arguments can they possibly present to their people to move them towards some social consensus that would allow repayment of the debt? I repeat: it's an impossible task—politically, socially, economically. I further repeat: these democratic leaders are not stupid men and women, and they will not cut their own political throats over some long-distance threat.

In recent times inflation rates have reached astonishing levels in certain Central and South American states—in Bolivia, for example, which drifts from one disaster to another, inflation was 2,300% several years ago; in Argentina, 675%; in Brazil, 194.7%; and in Perú, 105.8%. (Some of these figures improved after the newly-elected democratic governments imposed wage-and-price controls, particularly in Argentina and Brazil.) How can any sane person or government demand that these countries reduce inflation rates, balance their budgets, and also pay astronomical interest on their debts—all in a single year? It's insane. If I walked into one of your American banks, and proposed such a scenario to an officer there, I would be laughed out of the place.

These figures that I've been citing on Latin American resources transferred overseas are based exclusively on what has been reported by these countries officially, as interest payments and profits. But we also have to consider the hidden flight of personal capital into foreign banks, a figure which by its very nature is almost impossible to estimate. It is known, however, that tens of billions of dollars were sent from Venezuela to the United States in the last several years, and that the same thing happened in Argentina. In México, where the country has been severely affected by a drop in international oil prices, resulting in an inevitable and continuous devaluation of the peso, tens of billions of dollars were sent by wealthy Mexicans who have no faith in their own currency to the United States. In fact, the problem became so severe that the Mexican government was forced to impose currency controls on the conversion of pesos into dollars. Unfortunately, much of this sort of thing goes on through unofficial channels, and while it is unmeasurable with any accuracy, I am assured that more cash continues to flow through such open economic wounds than is ever transferred via official sources.

What has happened to these three countries has also been occurring throughout Latin America, for very logical, simple, and understandable reasons: when the currency of any Latin American country is seen to be devaluating at an accelerating rate, the people there immediately lose confidence in it, and begin transferring whatever resources they have to currencies they perceive as more stable. Were I in a similar situation, I would probably do the same. Fortunately, we do not have such problems in Cuba.

DYMALLY: I will agree with you that Latin America's debt is undoubtedly large, particularly in Brazil, México, and Venezuela, and possibly unmanageable. You seem to imply, however, that the real debt is larger than official figures which have been reported in the news and in government publications.

CASTRO: Well, I'm not sure. Financial experts have cited figures of $105 billion for Brazil, $100 billion for México, and $35 billion for Venezuela, but none of these figures are lower than the ones given in the offical data of the international economic agencies.

Some countries, such as Argentina, are using maybe half of their exports just to pay the interest on their debt. Bolivia uses roughly three-fifths for this purpose; México, about a third; Perú, also a third; Brazil, the same; and Chile, almost half—even though many of these nations struggle financially when more than 20% of their exports are absorbed by debt payments. Twenty percent seems to be the key demarcation level; those forced to expend more than that amount seem to be in bad economic shape generally.

What do these figures actually mean? Real economic development in Latin America has slowed to a crawl or even regressed in the last decade, as indicated by the fact that the gross national product of these countries as a whole dropped between 1981-1984. Uruguay, for example, regressed by 13.9%; Argentina by 6%; Chile by 5.4%; and Venezuela, in spite of that country's enormous economic resources and potential, by 6.1 percent. Since population increased during these years, the per capita gross national product dropped even more—in Bolivia, by 24.6%; in Costa Rica, by 14.1%; in Chile, by 11.2%; in México, by 6.3%; in Argentina, by 11.8%; in Venezuela, by 16.2%; and in Uruguay, by 16.2%. In the case of Venezuela, the per capita GNP dropped not only between 1981-1984, but also in the three preceding years, plummeting an additional 24%. The depth of the crisis is reflected in the fact that each country's industrial production actually declined during this period. Several of these states, recognizing the abyss opening up before them, are making truly impressive efforts to confront the situation. Three of the largest are:

Brazil, which exported $20.081 billion in goods in 1982, and increased that figure by almost $7 billion in just 2 years. Simultaneously, it reduced imports during the same period from $19.395 billion to $14.36 billion.

México, which exported $22.081 billion in goods in 1982, and increased that figure by a $1.5 billion two years later. It reduced annual imports from $14.434 billion in 1982 to $10 billion in 1984.

Argentina, which increased its exports from $7.622 billion in 1982 to $8.7 billion in 1984, and reduced imports from $4.859 billion in 1982 to $4.27 billion in 1984.

By making real efforts to increase their exports and drastically reduce their imports—to levels that are nearly untenable for their economies—these countries managed to obtain more favorable trade balances at great internal sacrifice. Brazil had a positive balance of $12.6 billion; México, $13.5 billion; and Argentina, $4.43 billion. All of these plusses were the result of tremendous efforts which practically exhausted these countries' stocks of raw materials, and which probably adversely affected the maintenance of their industrial infrastructures. What happened to the money earned from such backbreaking efforts? It all went to service the interest on these countries' debts.

Overall, Latin America transferred about $26.7 billion in financial resources abroad last year. In just two years, from 1983-1984, cash and intangibles from Latin America amounting to $56.7 billion were sent overseas. Ironically enough, it is the underdeveloped, Third World countries which are financing the economic development of the rich, industrialized countries of both North America and Europe. The money is gone forever: there is no possible way of ever retrieving it, or of recapturing lost opportunities and lost time.

The growth rate of the debt has recently declined, falling below the record level of 24% reached in 1981. There's a reason for this: no one wants to lend these countries any more money. But, even so, for one reason or another, Latin America's debts have continued to grow at an average annual rate of 5.5%. In the next 10 years, the interest on these sums—even if they are held at more or less the same level—will still average $40 billion a year.

Twenty-five years ago, when the Alliance for Progress was created, President Kennedy proposed a program of economic cooperation to meet Latin America's social problems and developmental needs, calling for $20 billion to be invested there over a period of 10-15 years. The idea arose as a reaction to the Cuban Revolution, seeking to avoid the creation of conditions that would be propitious for other communist revolutions in the region.

Now, the economically underdeveloped countries of this hemisphere, with twice the population and triple the social problems, will be giving the industrialized countries $40 billion annually as interest on their debts. In 10 years, they will pay out $400 billion—20 times more than Kennedy suggested investing over a 10-year period to "solve" Latin America's economic and social problems. A quarter century ago, there were half as many people and far fewer evident social ills in Central and South America. International economic growth was accelerating. There were fewer world crises that would affect Latin America. And these nations' export products had much greater purchasing power.

The political, economic, and social structures of Latin America cannot bear the burden of constantly-increasing restrictions and sacrifices.

Not long ago, when the International Monetary Fund first imposed its "reform" measures, there were repercussions in the Dominican Republic, a country which has had a relatively stable political history under a constitutional regime. Rising prices, triggered by the devaluation of the Dominican peso (which had originally been at par with the U.S. dollar, but was now reduced to a half of its former value), caused a popular uprising. The government's response was to order the army and the police to put down the demonstrations. The result, according to official figures, was 50 dead and 300 wounded. Many people say the real figure was larger. A few weeks ago, new demands by the International Monetary Fund led to the imposition of an exchange rate of three Dominican pesos per dollar on all import products, including fuel. The government, acting before the people did, once again ordered the army and the police to occupy the cities and crush the people's incipient protests. This has unnecessarily created great tension in the Dominican Republic.

A similar situation occurred in Panamá, not long after the new government was inaugurated. The new regime imposed a 7% tax on certain services, and postponed previously agreed upon wage increases for doctors and teachers. Hundreds of thousands took to the streets, but there was fortunately no repression by the government, and consequently no victims of repression, due to the progressive attitude of the National Guard. The Guard was instrumental in regaining Panamá's sovereignty over the Canal, and enjoys close ties with the populace—it has shown great reluctance in the past to fire on them. As a result, the measures were rescinded. These strictures weren't imposed by the IMF to "solve" Panamá's serious economic difficulties, which are similar to those of other Latin American countries; rather, they were simply attempts by a concerned government to balance its budget and to create the minimum conditions which they knew would be required by the IMF to renegotiate its debts.

In Bolivia, inflation rose at a rate of 2,300% in 1984, creating a situation which completely paralyzed the country. Tens of thousands of miners (armed with sticks of dynamite), workers, students, and farmers mobilized in the countryside, blocked the highways, and demanded wage increases, price controls, food provisions, and similar measures. How does a government respond to this kind of crisis? What can anyone, even an official with a popular following, do to alleviate the underlying causes of the unrest? The answer, of course, is that no one, myself included, can see any way Bolivia will emerge from its morass unscathed.

The curious thing is that these disparate events have occurred almost spontaneously in response to very similar stimuli.

DYMALLY: Some of my more conservative colleagues in the U.S. House of Representatives have said that the Latin American debt crisis is self-imposed—that is, no one forced these countries to borrow money at the terms specified, no one made them sign the agreements, no one forced them to take the money. Why should Americans worry about what happens south of the border? Doesn't Latin America have both a moral and legal obligation to meet its debts, just as other countries do?

CASTRO: No. And let me tell you why. Traditionally, those who needed money, for whatever reason, have gone to banks to secure loans. But in recent years, the practice has been reversed. Banks have amassed huge sums by scooping up, among other things, the financial surpluses of the oil-producing countries during the petroleum boom of the 1970s. Banks make money by lending money and earning interest. A decade ago the American banks, dissatisfied with the profits they were earning domestically, began searching for new clients abroad. They were extraordinarily successful. The situation is analogous to being approached by a stranger on the street and being offered a thousand dollars, no strings attached, no credit checks. Who's going to refuse such an offer? The average man (or the average Third World country), who is barely scraping by—or worse—will take the money and worry about paying it back later.

Of course these countries shouldn't have borrowed so heavily on their futures. They were foolish to do so. Still, the fact remains that, 20 or 25 years ago, Latin America had practically no overseas debt. Today, it owes $360 billion to foreign creditors. Where did the money go? Part of it was spent on weapons. In Argentina, for example, tens of billions of dollars were spent by military governments on tanks, planes, and fancy uniforms. The same thing happened in Chile and in other countries with large military infrastructures. Part of the money was embezzled or stolen, or was reinvested in foreign banks, frequently in Switzerland or in the United States. Some of it was simply squandered, as graft, bribes, largess, or just swallowed up in the inefficiencies of local bureaucracies. Part was used by some countries to offset the high cost of fuel and petroleum products. Finally, some small part actually was spent on real economic development to benefit the poor or to build up industry.

You talk about the moral responsibility these countries have to repay their debts. When you speak of nations, you're actually talking about the people who make up those nations: the workers, the farmers, the students, the middle class (*e.g.*, the doctors, engineers, teachers, and other professionals). Tell me, how have these little people benefited from $360 billion squandered on weapons, graft, or overpriced energy? What did they get from the overvaluation of the American dollar, or the increasingly high interest that western banks added to their original loans. Other than the few "fat cats" who actually arranged the transactions, the vast majority of the citizens of those countries received absolutely nothing. Who pays the piper? The people, of course. They pay, as they have always paid, through reduced or devalued wages, reduced or devalued incomes, and a vast scaling down of their financial hopes for the future. Where is the morality in imposing measures which will result either in a bloodbath, or in severe economic disturbances, civil unrest, military putsches, or even direct foreign intervention, as has been the case during this century in Nicaragua and the Dominican Republic? The people must protest, because they are being forced to repay a debt which they never directly approved, and which has brought them no tangible (and few intangible) benefits.

That's why I say that payment of this debt is both an economic and political impossibility. You would have to terrorize the people to force them into the necessary sacrifices. Any democratic process that tried to impose such things by force would quickly be destroyed or rendered impotent by the civil unrest it provoked. Such a solution would also be immoral, for reasons I've already stated.

The truly moral thing to do would be to outright cancel the debt, something which would benefit billions of people immediately, as opposed, say, to spending a similar amount on weapons—chemical weapons, nuclear bombs, biological warfare, aircraft carriers, battleships, strategic missiles, or "Star Wars." You must realize that this is not just a Latin American thing; I'm also talking about the debts of Africa and Asia, directly affecting the lives of some 70% of mankind. What seems truly immoral to me, as a leader of a Third World nation, is to force the common people of the world to go hungry, to live in poverty, to exist under the most terrible conditions, just to finance a meaningless and endless arms race between the East and the West. The billions spent on these enormously expensive and counterproductive doomsday weapons can only lead to the killing of hundreds of millions of people and perhaps the extinction of mankind. So, you tell me what is more moral: the outright cancellation of a debt which can never be collected anyway, or a reduction in one year's profits earned by the western military-industrial complex, and an end to the possibility of humanity's *götterdämmerung*?

DYMALLY: This seems to me an oversimplification of a very complex process. Are you saying that all of these loans, millions upon millions of dollars, were just frittered away through greed, inefficiency, and venality?

CASTRO: Much of it went for weapons and other military hardware. You must remember that most of the regimes on the receiving end were military dictatorships, and that the reasons they gave for borrowing the sums were ostensibly to fight communists or internal terrorists. Their motives were rarely questioned. Some of the generals became rich as a result—some of the money was deliberately stolen and deposited overseas in American or Swiss banks. The bankers didn't really care—for supposedly hard-nosed businessmen, they were surprisingly blasé about their investments. They were flush with funds accruing from deposits made by the big oil-exporting countries; there was so much money just floating around, in fact, that the banks began throwing loans at Third World countries, each trying to outdo their fellows in drumming up business. It would all be comical if it weren't so sad. The terms proposed provided, of course, for interest rates much lower than those common today, to be repaid with dollars worth much less than today. Unfortunately, all the agreements included clauses that allowed higher interest rates to be charged if the world economic situation changed, which is, of course, precisely what happened. What Latin America could not reasonably have foreseen, however, was that the value of the American dollar would increase to such unsupportable heights of fantasy. I cannot really see that the current situation benefits the U.S. any more than it does the Third World.

To recap, some of the money may have been invested in more or less useful ways; some was squandered on absurd, anti-nationalistic policies that were ruinous for local industry; some was lost to graft or military expenditures; and some was reinvested overseas.

ELLIOT: Yes, but isn't it true that some of this money did directly benefit the people of Latin America?

CASTRO: Of course. Some industrial equipment was purchased and installed. Some roads were built (particularly, in Brazil), and other improvements were made to the infrastructures of these nations (*e.g.*, hydroelectric projects and so forth). But at what cost? The bottom line is this: Latin America's assumption of an enormous burden of debt did not simultaneously result in the creation of an industrial or social utopia. Quite the contrary, in fact.

When I was talking earlier about how inflation prompts the flight of capital, I explained that a 175.4% inflation rate in Central and South America in 1984 resulted in a general loss of confidence in each of these countries' national currencies. Under such conditions, anyone who has money and wants to protect it will immediately change it into dollars and deposit it in U.S. banks. This is what México tried to prevent recently with its currency controls. Even though some of these states have seen the danger and have taken such steps, there are always ways of circumventing such regulations, legally or illegally. Nearly all of the countries in Latin America have an underground economy that offers a truer (and always cheaper) rate of exchange, sometimes varying by as much as two or three to one. For example, several Dominicans have told me that anyone with Dominican currency can get dollars without difficulty, either through their own banks or on the streets, always on the streets. You gentlemen are men of the world—you know this.

When people lose confidence in their own currency, those in higher income brackets take the equivalent of $50,000, $100,000, $500,000, or even $1 million in their national currencies, exchange it, deposit it in U.S. banks at high interest rates, and have their "futures" guaranteed. They don't usually spend too much time worrying about what effect this might have on their own economies.

Although such countries tend to pay higher domestic interest rates, precisely in order to attract money and to prevent the flight of capital, the present high levels of inflation in several Latin American states make it necessary to use a computer to get weekly estimates (or daily, as is the case in Bolivia) of how much the national currency has been devalued. Consequently, people from such nations who have the alternative of exchanging their devalued money for the foreign currency of a country that pays stable, long-term, relatively high interest rates will always do so. Latin American countries with underdeveloped economies are beset by such traps on all sides.

Of course, all countries are affected, to a greater or lesser degree, by the flight of capital to the United States, even the U.S. itself, which has suddenly found itself in recent years heavily indebted to other countries. The very attractiveness of your country as a safe haven for dollars has resulted in a flood of oil and investment funds deluging your financial institutions and markets, to the point where American industry is becoming increasingly owned by foreign interests. I find it terribly ironic that the most militaristic American president in generations (Ronald Reagan) has done more to harm the basic interests of your country, through ill-considered policies, failure of vision, lack of understanding, and an inability to spend his limited resources wisely, than any U.S. leader since Warren G. Harding.

The problem of capital disappearing overseas has also affected your allies, Europe and Japan, who, in 1983, invested $40 billion in U.S. industry and banks, partly as a response to the high interest being paid there. This in turn resulted from your government's massive expansion of its military forces without a corresponding willingness to pay for the expansion (so-called deficit financing). I understand that between $4-$5 billion was transferred in one year from the Federal Republic of Germany, a great industrial power, to the United States, just because interest rates were 4.5 points higher in America. With the fiscal fantasies your president is so fond of touting, it's no wonder that cash is flowing to the United States from all quarters. During 1983, $170 billion from foreign sources was invested in stocks and bonds in the United States. America's huge budgetary and trade deficits, amounting to $200 billion and $150 billion each annually, can only be financed by the rest of the world. I would think that even Mr. Reagan could understand the simple financial facts of life: when basic U.S. industries and financial institutions become wholly or partially owned by foreign masters, whose political or social aims may not coincide with those of the American government or its citizens, the United States may have to choose between losing its shirt or losing its freedom of action.

If we see such immense sums moving regularly from such highly industrialized countries as Japan and Germany (not to mention Spain, Italy, France, and England, all of them industrial powers), what can you expect in countries whose pathetically (by comparison) weak economies are struggling for development against a myriad of economic and social problems? How can Latin America defend itself against policies which are so adversely affecting the more developed industrial powers, who are presumably better able to defend themselves?

There are other factors at work here also. One of them—the really decisive one—is the unequal balance of trade between Latin America and the West. This is not just a modern phenomenon, of course—economists have traced it accurately over the past four decades. It began in colonial times, with the Spanish colonies being raped for their gold, slaves, and footstuffs; Spain got rich while the Americas were drained of their resources. We need to analyze the economic forces generating these imbalances so we can better understand their mechanisms, particularly as they affect commerce between the developing and the industrialized countries. Constantly rising prices for equipment, machinery, and the other finished products we import from the West, combined with the declining purchasing power of Latin America's basic exports, have produced enormous—and unfair—trade imbalances.

The purchasing power of products generated by Third World countries as a whole, including petroleum, dropped almost 22% between 1980 and 1984. In real terms this means that a given quantity of materials produced in Latin American for export to the industrialized states would buy 100 trade units in 1980, but only 78 units in 1984.

This is very important. If Latin America's exports in 1984 were worth roughly $95 billion, the nearly 22% drop in purchasing power would, in itself, mean a loss to us of almost $20 billion. You can say that this is a paper loss only, but what it really means is that the West not only plays the game of high-stakes international finance, but it also controls the rules, and seems quite willing to change the rules when it thinks no one can stop it. To name names, what can President Alfonsín (of Argentina) do to stem the flow of dollars from his country? How can he possibly control the deterioration of his country's balance of trade, when Ronald Reagan, who has much greater political, military, and financial power at his fingertips, has not been able to control yours?

Latin America also lost heavily during the period of high interest rates in the late 1970s and early 1980s—rates that were significantly higher than those in effect when the original debts were contracted for. Your bankers assumed that high prices and high interest rates would remain a fixed part of our financial futures, and because of this erroneous assumption, we lost more than $10 billion annually just in interest surcharges over a 5-8-year period.

We also lost heavily when the dollar was overvalued, during those same years. Loans that were worth, say, $100 billion in 1978 had to be paid back in American dollars worth 30% more in the early 1980s. Suddenly our debt increased by $30 billion, almost literally overnight, plus, of course, the additional interest on that sum.

When one begins adding these sums together, the amounts grow to staggering numbers: I estimate that Latin America was stripped of more than $45 billion in 1984 just for "minor" changes in the financial rules which you control. This total can be broken down into its individual components, thusly: $20 billion for deterioration in the purchasing power of our goods; $10 billion for interest surcharges; $10 billion for capital reinvested overseas, instead of at home, where it's most needed; and $5 billion (a conservative estimate) for the overvaluation of the dollar. When we add to this the "normal" interest on the debt, in just one year Latin America has transferred some $70 billion it could ill afford to the relatively rich, developed parts of the world, to countries which don't really need it. We were forced to pay $50 billion of this amount in cash, because, of course, our credit is no longer any good! It was certainly good enough when they were begging us, hats in hand, to take their crisp, new dollar bills.

Latin America cannot stand this continuing drain on the continent's resources for very long without risking financial collapse, and I submit that it is not in your best interests to allow this to happen. The long-term political and social stability of these states depends on their ability to keep their citizens happy. It's not a choice between communism or capitalism, but between functional government and chaos. Under both systems, and according to every religious or ethical system I've ever encountered, stealing is a crime, an affront to man and God alike. To demand that the poor maintain the living standards of the rich is just plain immoral, at least by my code of ethics. These policies are insupportable, unfair, unjust, and indefensible. There's a saying you Americans have: you can't get blood out of a turnip, and I'm telling you the simple, obvious truth when I say that you will never collect this money without physically occupying the states in question; and even you do not have the resources—or the will—to contemplate such action.

Deterioration in trade terms between the industrialized West and the Third World has been obvious for decades, to the point where the Movement of Non-Aligned Countries has gone on record as opposing it; the subject was also debated in the United Nations, where the need for a New International Economic Order was made clear. The trend in the West is toward economic protectionism, plus the dumping of subsidized products into regions which basically can't defend themselves—such as Latin America.

Alfonsín can't be blamed for inheriting this crisis, nor can Sanguinetti, Tancredo Neves, Alan García, Belisario Betancur, Febres Cordero, or Siles Suazo. They face a terrible dilemma. Pinochet is in a different category, since his fraticidal *coup*, and his enthusiastic support of and cooperation with the fascist elements in the world, brought on many of his economic ills. Panamá and Costa Rica aren't to blame, nor are México or Venezuela. In fact, I can honestly say that none of these states, including Chile, welcome their present dilemma, and that all of them would do almost anything to escape it.

So, we must solve the problem of the debt—and do so without delay. If this doesn't happen—and soon—none of the democratic institutions so newly established in Latin America (and so loudly praised by President Reagan) can survive, because the same economic crises that drove the military officers from public administration, in such countries as Argentina, Uruguay, and Brazil, will inevitably drag the democratically-elected governments that have replaced them into a whirlwind of political tensions, social upheaval, and economic problems.

General Pinochet's fascist methods, and the Dominican Republic's draconian imposition of the International Monetary Fund's financial measures, cannot be repeated elsewhere, given the political, economic, and social realities in most Latin American states—nor are their new leaders about to accept them.

The crisis will continue to grow until some real solutions are found. It is simply an illusion to believe that the problem can be solved with mere palliatives, debt renegotiations, or other traditional formulas. Latin American politicians of all stripes have changed their attitudes. There are fewer and fewer conservatives in this hemisphere, because many of those who have traditionally been considered "right-wingers," and many of the organizations and parties which have been called "conservative," are now aware of how deep and serious these debt problems has become. You can talk to them all you want about the Chicago School, of tearing down tariff barriers, of letting their countries' nascent industries compete with the industries of the developed countries, but who will listen? Not

I—and certainly not President Reagan, a man who knows nothing about either economics or about Latin America. Now, even the conservatives in Latin American feel bitter and defrauded. I'm not even talking about the many intellectuals, filmmakers, artists, writers, professionals, students, or ordinary workers, all of whom represent a broad range of other political parties running from center to left in Central and South America. These people don't have to be convinced by any words from me.

I have made a point of repeating these words on many other occasions to visitors and journalists from Japan, Europe, and many other capitalist and socialist countries. The problem of the debt must be resolved, and the economic crisis must be overcome, if we are to prevent a general social upheaval in Latin America. I believe that such widespread economic unrest would inevitably result in social revolution in Latin America. Is this what you really want?

ELLIOT: Looking at it from the other side, however, hasn't Latin America's inability to repay its debts undermined its ability to get new loans which it badly needs for development?

CASTRO: New loans? Why do these nations need new loans? If they're already paying $40 billion a year now—and they'll have to pay $40 billion annually even if the debt stays the same—that's $400 billion in just 10 years, payments which can only be made at great personal sacrifice. I see a real problem here just convincing the people of Central and South America to do this much. They certainly don't need new obligations. They can lend themselves $40 billion (or $400 billion) for internal development. The people will see the need for such sacrifices, and for implementing austerity measures necessary for their own national welfare. But I sure can't see them making such sacrifices to promote backwardness, decrease per capita income, and reduce their GNP. But perhaps you can persuade them otherwise!

You must understand something—western banks can't offer the people of Latin America any more than they can offer themselves. For example, if Brazil is paying $12 billion a year in interest on its debt, it certainly doesn't need to borrow more; if it had invested that $12 billion ten years ago, it would now have $120 billion available for development purposes. México, with its huge internal monetary restrictions, is somehow managing to export $23.5 billion worth of products while importing just $10 billion, taking the difference, in effect, out of the living standards of its people; it could and should invest the difference toward its own industrial development instead of paying the interest on its debt. That would mean some $100 billion replowed back into the Mexican economy in 10 years. If Argentina is paying out $5 billion annually, the aggregate would amount to $50 billion in the next decade.

Who will lend those countries new sums for their internal development? If anyone did, Latin America would soon be paying $60 billion a year in interest instead of $30 billion. Its economy would have to grow just to keep paying more interest to western banks. The situation can be compared to that of Sisyphus, in Greek legend, who was doomed to push a large stone uphill for all eternity, a stone that would always roll down again before reaching the top. We of the Third World continue to push with all of our might against a massive debt that continues to grow, in spite of our best efforts, but it just keeps rolling down that hill again.

I've cited many examples, but the same is true of Venezuela, Colombia, Ecuador, Perú, Uruguay, and almost all the other Latin American countries. Instead of lending them more money, why not allow them to use their own resources for their own development, purportedly the rationale behind the original loans. Reprisals against these countries would be forbidden in a civilized world. The industrialized world can't really manage without the undeveloped nations' trade, and particularly their raw materials and minerals. Why not make them partners instead of chattel?

Can you imagine any of the western states getting along without chocolate, coffee, tea, or cashew nuts? Or nutmeg, cloves, peanuts, sesame seeds, pineapples, and coconuts (not to mention coconut oil for their mild and fragrant soaps)? Life would be very sad indeed for the West if raw steel, copper, aluminum, and other minerals and chemicals suddenly ceased being shipped. Increasingly, this is a world in which all states must depend at least partially on the others to make their economies work.

The decision-making power no longer rests with the West. If I, the so-called renegade of Latin America, told you: "You must cooperate and play fair," 10 or maybe a hundred years would go by without them paying me the least bit of attention. But this debt represents nothing more than a systematic and historical plunder of the Third World by the West, something which cannot and will not continue—I repeat, the decision is now in the hands of Latin America and the other Third World states. They are morally entitled to suspend payments. This isn't something new, by the way: it's as old as Roman law. Loans, moratoriums, payments, and defaults all existed in the ancient world—sometimes decreed by the state, at other times by the debtors themselves. Of course, in those days Rome—which was as democratic as the United States, with a Senate much like your Senate, and a Capitol like the Capitol of the United States—immediately hauled debtors into court and declared them slaves. Enslavement as a punishment for penury has existed for millennia, almost to modern times. Even in the twentieth century, there are still a few countries where people who don't pay their debts are placed into bondage. Tell me, what good are all your fancy words about human rights and man's achievements when measured against the fact that the industrialized countries have economically enslaved billions of people throughout the world, in a legalized servitude which exploits them as mercilessly as if they were slaves. Today, the proles work almost exclusively for the benefit of the industrialized countries; they are, in effect, slaves without chains. The day is coming, however, when they may well decide to cast off those chains, and proclaim their freedom from their overseas masters.

This has happened many times in world history. At the end of the eighteenth century, the slaves in Haiti revolted against the French, and drove them out of Hispaniola. Later, slaves in the United States were freed by your President Lincoln. There have been many similar occurrences throughout the world. No one in recent times ever questions the necessity of freedom for all men. The overseas debt may become the chisel by which the economically enslaved peoples of the Third World finally break their chains.

The unilateral cancellation of the debt would be an utterly moral and absolutely unobjectionable proclamation of freedom. Latin American must throw away its credit cards, however painful that may be in the short term. They must, as you say, go "cold turkey." In the end, even the industrialized world would benefit, because the developing countries now would have greater buying power: instead of importing $10 billion worth of goods, for example, México could import $20 billion worth, or Argentina $8.5 billion worth instead of $4.2 billion. This would also be true of Brazil and the rest of the Latin American countries. Where else would they find finished products, goods, agricultural supplies, transportation, and industrial equipment, if not from the United States, Europe, and Japan? The Third World's buying power would increase every year by at least $80 billion—which, if well invested, would guarantee the sustained growth of their economies, assuming that the principles sanctioned by the United Nations were also applied. This would mean greater exports for the industrialized world, stability and growth for Latin America, and additional employment for everyone.

Unemployment is the curse of both the developed and underdeveloped states. By allowing the Latin American debt to be cancelled, the U.S. and its allies would ultimately increase employment and industrial profits, export more goods, invest the profits in sounder commercial ventures, both domestically and abroad, and recover much of the money theoretically lost by western banks to the Third World during the last decade. I'm not suggesting that these financial institutions must or even should go bankrupt. I'm also not implying that they must or should write off their investments. Finally, I'm not stating here that the American taxpayer must or should make up the difference through higher taxes. Rather, I'm making a very simple, very modest, very straightforward proposal: that the United States use a small percentage of its military budget—say, 12% or less—to insure the debts of its own financial institutions. In this way, neither the banks nor their depositors would lose; on the contrary, both would have their funds guaranteed by the highest authority in the land. The richest and most powerful industrial state the world has ever seen has the means to accomplish this—that is, if it has the will. If America can develop a "Star Wars" system, while barely giving a thought to the risks involved in a thermonuclear conflict (something that would destroy in one minute a hundred times more property than what is owed your banks); if, in short, the idea of universal suicide doesn't scare Ronald Reagan, then why should he fear something as simple as the cancellation of the Third World debt? What would you lose by trying? Only a small fraction of an already bloated military infrastruction, and I don't know anyone except Caspar Weinberger who thinks we haven't already spent enough on arms to keep even the smallest states in the world well supplied for the next 10 generations. My solution to the debt problem is both moral, reassuring, and healthful—it also links the Third World's economic problems with peace and international détente, something all countries want.

East or West, we want to end the arms race and reduce military spending, both to save the world and to save ourselves economically. This is one way of doing so while simultaneously helping those who need it most. In many ways it's just a simple accounting operation. It won't close a single factory, stop a single ship from sailing, or interfere with a single sales agreement. On the contrary, employment, trade, and industrial and agricultural output would inevitably increase worldwide. The only adverse effects would be on military spending, which does not provide food, clothing, education, health services, housing, or any other known benefit (including security) for anyone but the generals—and we have too many of those already, on both sides of the Cold War.

So this is what I suggest. And if it's a simple solution to the world's ills, it's not as simplistic as some western commentators would like to believe. It requires an act of good will by leaders to whom this does not come naturally. It does take into account everyone's interests, hurting no one and benefiting all. Perhaps it's too much to hope that something so easy would be readily adopted by the West, but then, I really don't understand you people sometimes. You're quite willing to waste $100 million annually supporting the Contras in their hopeless war against the legitimate government of Nicaragua, or to invade Grenada on the spur of the moment just because you don't like their duly-elected leaders. But you won't spend even a small sum to support your so-called allies in their direst economic crisis since the Great Depression. Grenada is a good example. You invaded an utterly defenseless state with a massive force of marines, set up your own government, and then left. Nothing has changed there except the people at the top: there is still massive unemployment (some 20-40 percent, depending on the source), great discontent, no hope for the average man to find work—in other words, the classic ingredients for another revolution. Maurice Bishop did not assume power in a vacuum—the people there saw him and his party as a way out of their interminable misery and poverty, much as the great mass of Cubans saw me in 1959. The same thing will happen again if conditions remain unchanged.

There is a lack of continuity here which I would find profoundly disturbing if I were a North American. The United States seems to have no understanding of the problems inherent in this part of the world, or, indeed, of its own national self interest in dealing with them. I can tell you both that forgiving the debt would be the best thing your country could do to improve its image in Latin America, not to mention doing some real good there, as opposed to just achieving certain short-term political aims. The people—and their leaders—would remember America's generosity for generations to come, and would be appropriately grateful and sympathetic to American foreign-policy ventures. Unfortunately—I'm resigned to the inevitable—your leaders have never really understood the meaning of the Cuban Revolution, and have never really listened to what I've been saying for the past quarter century. Whatever I advocate must be wrong, you say. So be it. "History will judge" the accuracy of my predictions.

DYMALLY: Some economists have said that the conditions imposed by the International Monetary Fund on the Third World constitute a blueprint for economic and political disaster; others maintain they're a necessary beginning for countries that have yet to put their own economic houses in order. What would you say?

CASTRO: They're a disaster, by whatever measurements you want to use. They've already caused an unprecedented economic crisis, one with wholly predictable consequences. Let me tell you, I know what the people of Latin America are thinking. I've talked to individuals from every social and economic stratum, men and women holding diverse political views from both the right and the left. Their near unanimous consensus is that the debt cannot be repaid, that it is just part of an unjust and intolerable economic relationship that has been imposed on Latin America by the West over a long period of time. One way or another, they agree, this situation must and will change. The International Monetary Fund, whose policies have caused such immense harm to the Third World in recent years, may ultimately deserve our gratitude, because it has brought the crisis to a head, forcing Latin America to find solutions that were not even contemplated a few years ago. History tells us that major problems will not be solved until they reach crisis proportions. Mankind has never had sufficient foresight to act otherwise. The IMF and the economic system it represents will ultimately spark a revolution in the Third World, one which will resolve not only the debt, but also a long-term system of unjust and intolerable economic servitude imposed by a handful of rich, industrialized states on the hundred or so poor nations in which three-quarters of the world's population live. So the problem will not be resolved through some kind of miracle, through proclamations, ideas, arguments, or someone's kindly persuasion, or even through subversion. It's the crisis itself that will inevitably lead to some resolution, as pleasant or unpleasant a prospect as that may be for the West.

As you know, the United States achieved its independence only when forced to face a series of unpleasant choices by Great Britain. Similarly, you did not abolish slavery until a crisis occurred in 1861. In more recent times, President Roosevelt's New Deal—which, by the way, saved capitalism—was his response to the Great Depression of the 1930s. You might recall that America's economy never seemed healthier or more prosperous than just before the eve of the catastrophe. During the first World War, a massive economic and social crisis sparked the revolution in Russia; similar problems prompted independence movements in India and other Third World states, and the revolution in China. The socialist uprisings in Europe, and the end of the colonial system, followed the chaos of World War II.

If you analyze the history of mankind, you will see that this has always been true. Can you reasonably expect anything different from the economic, social, and ecological catastrophes currently afflicting the people of Latin America? Won't the debt trigger even greater changes in international economic relations? I have no doubt whatever that these problems will either be solved by reasonable men or great social upheavals will take place that will lead to widespread revolutionary changes.

Ultimately, as a token of gratitude, we might even erect a monument to the International Monetary Fund, and later add a second one for Ronald Reagan. The sense of crisis—all the policies which caused it—are helping to unite the disparate governments of the Third World, irrespective of ideology, into one loud voice insistently demanding a change in the established economic structure. I am convinced of it. I am absolutely certain that we are witnessing a grass-roots revolution that will rock the very foundations of the economic establishment. The International Monetary Fund has run out of arguments to refute the facts, the figures, and the realities of the situation. All of their theses, all of their traditional formulas, all of their prescriptions, are in turmoil.

The representatives and theoreticians of this venerable institution could collect together Latin American leaders, academics, professionals, economists, and left- and right-wing politicians into one big theater and present them with their theses and theories and explanations of how the problems we're talking about should be solved; and maybe those tight-lipped men—who, 25 or 30 years ago, would have welcomed them with applause and brass bands—will reward them with no more than cold, ironic smiles. No one in Latin America believes them anymore. The Brandt Commission was probably the last effort to introduce real reform, and to put a bit of flesh and common sense onto the skeleton of the old system, a system which had been created at the Bretton Woods Conference at the end of World War II for the express purpose of dominating and exploiting the natural and human resources of Third World countries. But no one in the Third World has paid it any attention.

So it's not just a matter of a new awakening. You become aware of the problem when the problem exists in its fullest dimensions and seriousness. Until then, everything is mere theoretical speculation—the noble work of visionaries. Now the real crisis has reached these levels. The western economic system has fallen into its own trap, and its enlightened economic advisers—the brilliant "wizards" who worked these fabulous "miracles" we've already talked about—are creating the basis for a major economic tragedy in the United States and elsewhere.

I'd like to say just one additional thing. Recently, the wire services carried a rather unusual piece of news: Reagan was the first to arrive—very early in the morning—at the New York Stock Exchange. That's because there were reports that the U.S. economy's growth during the first quarter of 1985 was beginning to lose ground in the international market. President Reagan was at the Stock Exchange to boost the dollar, to inspire confidence in the American economy. Since all this business is to a great degree "magical," there was a real need to conjure up the spirits. In other words, if the money to run the American economy doesn't come from such traditional sources as labor, production, productivity, or gold, it must be created from thin air. He had to perform, in effect, something akin to a religious rite, to protect the U.S. economy from the shifting tides of misfortune. Maybe Herbert Hoover's ghost was haunting the Stock Exchange, and the evil spirits had to be exorcised.

DYMALLY: During this interview, you have proposed one possible solution to the debt crisis. How has Latin America responded to your ideas?

CASTRO: I've spoken about this problem for quite some time now—for example, at the United Nations in October, 1979. In my speech to that organization, I called for the cancellation of the debts of the least developed countries, and easier payment terms for the other, more developed nations of the Third World. I also mentioned the need for additional financial resources amounting to $300 billion for developmental assistance in the decade 1980-1990, if the programs that the United Nations has proposed for that part of the world were to be implemented. Many of these problems—those of unequal trade, protectionist measures, and other issues—were defined in 1979, before the great economic crisis of the 1980s had yet occurred. The present situation is very different.

I set forth those same theses in New Delhi in 1983, at the Summit Conference of the Movement of Non-Aligned Countries, and at other international meetings; but—I repeat—with significant differences, based on two elements: firstly, the crisis hadn't yet reached its most critical point; and, secondly, we were drawing up possible solutions, for discussions, as well as listing appropriate measures which could be taken, arguing and reasoning over them, and requesting time. This was necessary: the United Nations' goals have not been met. The gap between the industrialized and Third World countries is widening; cooperation is necessary between all parties. Resources are needed for development. I summarized all of this at great length. I believe my statements were fair and balanced but their importance was relative, because—I repeat—the crisis hadn't yet reached its fullest limits. We should analyze what has happened between 1979, when I first made these proposals, and the spring of 1985. The data telling what actually happened in each Latin American country are readily available.

On the other hand, while I can talk and many will listen, the power to make decisions was always before in the hands of the industrialized countries. They could turn (and have turned) a deaf ear to the problem. The situation is now totally different; the crisis has progressed, and we Latin American leaders can do very little except respond to the needs of our people. Now it is we who must take action. The industrialized nations will have to accept what the Third World decides, or risk a bloodbath and/or a total collapse of the world economic order.

With respect to Latin America's response, I can only tell you that my proposals have awakened great interest in all of these nations and in all social sectors. What will the answer be? Even if I hadn't said a word—and my words now have minimal value, since

the time has come for decisions and action—these countries would
have to find an answer to the debt. They will ultimately reach the
same conclusions, one way or the other. I don't have any doubts
that they will follow a path similar to mine, because there is no alternative. No one at this point needs much persuasion. I am merely
stating facts: what is happening, why it has happened, and what
will happen with proposed solutions.

Thus, the ideas, analyses, and suggestions I have offered are
merely the products of a grim reality. They certainly don't represent, as your government has indicated, the ravings of a lunatic, or
the wild imaginings and fantasies of a Latin American surrealist.
Many other men and women in Central and South America have
been thinking about these same problems and have been coming to
the same conclusions on their own.

If I'm crazy, then most of the Third World is crazy, too. I
now feel much freer about speaking openly on these topics. I've
been talking about the debt since 1979—for 6 years now—and I've
been evolving my ideas all during that entire period. Nothing that
has happened in real life has in any way altered my views—or improved the situation any, for that matter. Fortunately, Cuba's economy has a more solid foundation for development; it doesn't depend
at all on the United States, which has blockaded us economically for
25 years. Cuba is less dependent generally on the western world's
economy, and we are less vulnerable to economic pressures and retaliation than the other Latin American countries, which are being
forced constantly to reschedule their debts to avoid outright default.
Their situation isn't the same as ours, but I'm convinced that many
public figures in Latin American and the Third World have already
reached these conclusions on their own, even though they may not
be in the position to state them as openly as I am doing here.

If you follow the international wire services, you will see Nyerere in Africa speaking out strongly about debt-related problems
and on Africa's tragic economic situation. He hasn't done this in
exactly the same terms, but he is, in essence, reflecting the same
concerns and the same urgent needs that I have just outlined. We
are all faced with a situation in which the affected countries have no
choice but to seek solutions other than those proposed by the West;
such solutions must necessarily lie in the same direction that I am
pointing. The debt simply cannot be paid under the terms demanded
by the lenders. You must remember that the American Revolution
was initially sparked by harsh British economic measures designed
to squeeze every last farthing from their American colonies. These
unjust taxes were ostensibly instituted to pay for the decades-long
war waged by England and France for control of the North American continent. When Patrick Henry proclaimed: "Give me liberty
or give me death," he was not only speaking of political freedom,

but of freedom from unjust taxation imposed by a geographically distant, politically unsympathetic, repressive government. Similarly, those governing Latin America now see their choices narrowed to the cancellation of the debt or political and economic death.

ELLIOT: What are the major stumbling blocks to the successful resolution of the debt wars?

CASTRO: So far, the United States and the other industrialized countries have tried to avoid the problem altogether by tackling it through separate discussions with each of the affected countries, and by making certain small concessions—such as the rescheduling of the debt, granting extensions for repayment of the original capital outlays, and evolving complicated formulas that don't really solve anything—which offer only brief, spasmodic relief from these countries' prolonged agony. Any real solution requires a truly radical formula—and not just for tackling the debt, which is only a part of the problem. If the debt were cancelled tomorrow, within a few years the same countries would once again decline to present economic levels or worse. In some cases, their situation is so difficult that the cancellation of the debt would hardly give them a breather.

I have already said that there are certain problems far worse than the debt: depressed prices, the flight of capital, excessive interest, the overvaluation of the dollar, protectionism, and commodity dumping. Together, they deprive Latin America of twice the resources which should be remitted for "normal" interest on the loans. If the problem of the debt is solved, and these problems remain, we will have achieved nothing.

The industrialized countries appear to have no rational, effective plan to address the debt crisis. Absolutely none. I believe that the main difficulty lies with the West's failure to understand the nature and seriousness of the problem. I'm not advocating *per se* new social revolution in these countries. I'm also not advocating the nationalization of foreign enterprises in Latin America, or anything else which your commentators might call "communistic." What I'm propounding are financial formulas which would benefit all of the underdeveloped (or even the developed) countries in the world. The cancellation of the debt, in the manner outlined, would be an important step toward ending the current international economic crisis. It would actually help foreign companies with investments in the Third World. And it would damage none of the creditor countries or their governments. On the contrary, the industrialized nations would experience higher levels of both employment and industrial output. The banks would survive intact, and western taxpayers would be protected from additional levies.

If this basic fact was understood by the West, I believe the path toward economic equity could be made much smoother, both through continuing dialogue, and by actual signed agreements between the industrialized and the Third World countries. As I said earlier, the only thing that need be sacrificed is an increasingly irrational arms race, that ever-frantic madness of weapons and war and waste of resources—and that, unfortunately, only to a very limited extent. If the New International Economic Order, already agreed to by the United Nations, is promulgated as an indispensable part of an economic package which includes cancellation of the debt, the natural complement to such a program would be a greater reduction in military expenditures. Most men would agree, I think, that reducing the danger of war, even to a small degree, would be beneficial to mankind.

I've spoken with dozens of people lately, including many Latin Americans, and I haven't met one person, of any ideological bent, of any political label, who wasn't absolutely convinced that this was correct.

If we fail in our quest for a negotiated agreement, what will happen? The answer is simple: the Third World countries will impose their own settlement. Essentially, the situation is as follows: it is materially impossible for these nations to pay the debt and its interest; therefore, it cannot be paid on the terms now stated. It would take rivers of blood to force the people to make the sacrifices this implies, for which they would receive nothing. No government, democratic or otherwise, would be strong enough to do this. I could not do it. We must find some common ground between creditors and debtors. We now have a temporary breathing period while world economic conditions are generally good, and while oil prices remain low benefitting everyone (except those countries which depend on oil for a substantial portion of their revenue). If we delay, even for a few years, until the next worldwide recession hits, the initiative will inevitably pass to the very nations that are being pressured to make these monstrous sacrifices.

If the debtor countries of the Third World are forced to suspend payments unilaterally, the industrialized countries will be left with few possible alternatives. A large-scale economic blockade, a military invasion of the defaulting countries, a new repartitioning of the world, to ensure, as in past centuries, guaranteed supply of raw materials and collection of the debt—these are simply impossible. Any rational person can understand this. An economic blockade of any country or group of countries would lead immediately to expressions of solidarity by those in similar straits, formation of economic cartels, and probably worldwide depression on an order greater than that of the 1930s.

44

The world is now one big family, and times are changing. Mankind has already abandoned certain of its madnesses; others—such as those we have discussed in the course of this interview—are doomed to extinction.

When I was in the fourth or fifth grade, and just beginning to study world geography—before I had any clear idea of what it was about—I must surely have thought that the world was flat, as men believed during the Middle Ages. Then I discovered many marvelous things: that the Earth was really round; that there was a sun around which it orbited; and that there were planets and stars and even a moon orbiting around our planet.

Later, I learned about the rivers, oceans, seas, gulfs, lakes, mountains, and other wonders of this world. Then I began learning about political geography. The maps of each continent were beautifully colored: the English colonies—in Africa, the Middle East, Asia, Oceania, India, Burma, Canada, New Zealand, and Australia—were in red. I remember this very well, and it had nothing to do with communism. That map was almost all red.

The color for France and its colonies was the next most extensive one: yellow covering the Caribbean, part of Africa, Asia, the Indian Ocean, and the Pacific Ocean. Countries that are well known today, such as Algeria, Vietnam, and Syria, were mere anonymous spots of yellow on those maps. Some of those spots, lost in the deep blue immensity of the oceans, remain a headache for France to this day. A large part of Africa was yellow, and it had nothing to do with China.

There were many other colors: orange, brown, green, gray, etc. You saw countries as small as Portugal, Belgium, Holland, and Denmark, mere specks on the map of Europe, occupying large sections of the world, in which the home countries could fit many times over. Mozambique covered a considerable portion of southwest Africa, painted in the green of Portugal. Green was also the color of Angola, another large colony; and of the tiny islands of Cape Verde, Sao Tome, and Principe, plus sections of India and Oceania. That small European country, one of the most primitive of western Europe, where many people didn't even know how to read or write, owned, at that time, extensive overseas territories.

Then came the Dutch, with big territories in the East Indies. Belgium had the vast Congo; Denmark, the enormous expanse of Greenland, covered with ice and almost uninhabitable, occupied more for prestige than any real material purpose. Even Spain, who once boasted that the sun never set on its immense dominions, still possessed several territories in Equatorial Guinea and Western Sahara, whose people are our Spanish-speaking brothers in Africa. These industrialized countries of the West had carved up the world among themselves and were owners both of the land and of the people. Even Mussolini waxed enthusiastic over his dreams of reestablishing the old Roman Empire. Libya, Somalia, and part of Ethiopia weren't enough for him. He invaded the only independent territory that was left in Africa, the remnants of the ancient Kingdom of Ethiopia. A large part of China and all of Korea bore the colors of the Rising Sun. This was presented to us as just another natural phenomenon in the world, like the mountains and the rivers. I never heard my teachers make the slightest critical analysis of these maps, and I was supposedly receiving a good education.

Years later, I came to understand that this was all an absurd madness, a great injustice, a terrible crime; and that colonialism has not only caused numerous wars and conflicts over the centuries, but that it was directly responsible for a systematic, continual repartition of the world's natural resources, including its greatest resource, man himself. However, nothing seemed more natural, moral, or fair to the civilized, Christian, western world, the world of our "great" thinkers and philosophers, than a system which benefited the few at the expense of the many. "Liberty," "equality," and "fraternity"—these were words which applied only to Europeans and other limited whites. It was very difficult for that kind of world to accept the fact that the Indians, Blacks, and Asians had minds, souls, or consciousnesses of their own. Socialism was still a distant idea: nothing disturbed the idyllic world of nascent, voracious capitalism, except, perhaps, the disquieting undercurrents of a rumbling conscience.

On the map, Latin America was shown as a group of independent countries. Later, I was able to see for myself just what kind of independence the Latin American countries really had.

The colonized countries had no idea, of course, how weak their masters were and what enormous potential power lay in their patriotism and national dignity. Feats such as those wrought by the people of Vietnam and Algeria hadn't yet taken place, although it's only fair to note that, by the end of the past century, Cuba had already shown that a small country could stand up to one of the mightiest European military powers.

How much has the population of the Third World grown in the last eight decades? How much has our political know-how, our sense of national dignity, our awareness of our own enormous potential, grown and multiplied?

I wonder if the creditor nations really want to apportion these countries among themselves again, if they would really dare to move militarily against the Third World, if they can even consider imposing an economic blockade against a country which is forced to suspend payments on its debt?

Any such attempt by the industrialized world would quickly result in its political and social isolation, with the remnants reduced to a small group of squabbling countries, each differing with the others over certain basic issues, none able to agree on a unified agenda. We have seen some of this bickering already. So, in point of fact, there isn't the slightest possibility that they could impose an economic blockade on, intervene in, reapportion these countries among themselves, or turn back the clock to the times when I was a fifth-grader in elementary school.

ELLIOT: Is unity possible, given the dissimilarity of governments in Latin America?

CASTRO: I think so. The economic crises will unite these countries much more than say, the War of the Malvinas (the Falkland Islands conflict). In that particular case, some of the Latin American states united behind Argentina's struggle against colonial pretensions, historic plunder, and an act of injustice dating back to the period when England was the most powerful empire in the world. The War of the Malvinas was indeed a war waged by a European country against a Latin American one, but it didn't directly affect the continent's vital economic interests. Except for certain aspects of patriotism, pride, and politics, Latin America had nothing to win or lose economically. Whatever solidarity that occurred was truly selfless. In the case of Latin America's economic crisis, however, the outcome is a matter of survival for all the countries of Latin America.

We have touched briefly on the Great Depression of the 1930s. The present crisis is far worse than the one which I experienced during my childhood. Except for oil, Latin America's export products have less purchasing power today than they had 50 years ago. Even if only go back 24 years, the purchasing power of our main traditional export products, including sugar, is in many cases only a third or a fourth of what it was at that time.

Let me give you an example. Twenty-four years ago, it took 200 tons of sugar to buy a 180-hp bulldozer. Today, it takes 800 tons of sugar at the world market price to buy that same bulldozer—and I'm not at all certain it's a better machine. Similarly, if you analyze coffee, cocoa, bananas, and the minerals Latin America exports, the number of products needed to purchase construction, transportation, agricultural, or industrial equipment from the industrialized states is 3-4 times greater now than it was then. Compared to 1950, the deterioration in trade relations is obvious, even to the uninitiated and enormously detrimental to the economy and health of the Third World.

What has changed in the last 50 years? Latin America's population in the 1930s was one-third less than what it is now; the resulting social pressures—overcrowding, disease, hunger—are far greater today than 5 decades ago—and these problems have been escalating. Thus, we now have 3-4 times as many people, and perhaps 10 times as many social problems, All of which must be supported with a declining economic infrastructure. The gap between the haves and have-nots internally and externally, is rapidly growing wider. At the time of the Great Depression, Latin America had practically no foreign debt. Now, we have a debt of $360 billion. A mathematical analysis of the situation—and common sense— shows that the debt can never be paid, that the affected countries are doomed to fall further and further behind until they default. This is so whether you analyze the situation as a whole or whether you examine each country individually; in some cases, it's more serious than in others, but it's serious enough in all, without exception, to cause great concern.

According to the latest official data gathered by the United Nations Economic Commission for Latin America and the Caribbean, Brazil owes $101.8 billion; México, $95.9 billion; Argentina, $48 billion; Venezuela, $34 billion; Chile, according to calculations that, in my opinion, are very conservative, $18.4 billion; Perú, $13.5 billion; Columbia, $10.8 billion; Costa Rica, a small country with a populaiton of approximately 2 million, $4.05 billion; Panamá, with a similar population, $3.55 billion; and Uruguay, $4.7 billion. These are conservative figures, since, according to reports by distinguished Uruguayan and Chilean friends, Uruguay's real debt is $5.5 billion, and Chile's may be as large as $23 billion. The official figures have been lowered for a variety of political reasons, but largely to disguise the real level of the debt. In many cases, it isn't easy for the international agencies—or even the governments of the countries themselves—to determine exact figures, because, in addition to controlled debts, there are a multitude of others made with private bodies, which often aren't reported.

ELLIOT: Let's assume that the debt crisis continues to worsen. How will this affect democratic political institutions in Latin America?

CASTRO: Ultimately, whoever is in power, irrespective of their political philosophy, irrespective of the kind of government in power, they will fall, no matter what they do. If it's Augusto Pinochet, for example, it would imply the end of Pinochet's government; if it's a government like the one recently elected in Uruguay, it could mean the end of democratic institutions in that country; in Brazil and Argentina, it could result in the opposition assuming power, or in new military dictatorships. This isn't a selective virus: it infects everyone—dictators, democrats, right-wingers, centrists, left-wingers— everyone. And, of course, I wouldn't complain too much if Pinochet's regime did suddenly disappear, nor, I think, would the people of Chile. What really hurts is that it could also mean the rapid erosion of all the democratic governments that have emerged from military rule over the past few years. Surely you don't want this.

However, if I had to guess, I don't really think we'll see new right-wing military *coups*. Rather, there will be social upheavals which will assume revolutionary characteristics with the possible participation of progressive, nationalist elements from the military. I believe that the armed forces are generally in open retreat from government, precisely because of the crisis. The Latin American countries have become so unmanageable that the military have abandoned the seat of power to the civilians. For the time being, they want nothing to do with the administration of the state, though this doesn't preclude the emergence of revolutionary movements within the military in some countries, as a result of the crisis. Whether it will be the civilians or the military or a combination of the two that assume responsibility, someone will have to tackle this problem and make hard decisions. Under these circumstances, anything could happen.

DYMALLY: Are you concerned that the industrialized world could blockade Latin America if any of these nations default?

CASTRO: Nothing the industrialized world does could be worse than what's happened already—and is still happening. In any event, it's a political impossibility in today's world. One or two countries could perhaps be blockaded—a whole continent could not. Neither can the entire Third World, for that would mean that the industrialized world would, in effect, be blockading itself from essential sources of goods and raw materials. What a few of the underdeveloped countries do will surely—with very few exceptions—be supported by the rest.

ELLIOT: Let's assume that Latin America approved your plan. Won't the creditor banks adopt strong measures to counter it?

CASTRO: What can they do? The Latin American states, because of their political importance, their combined size and population, their location, their huge debts, their terrible economic and social problems and the commiserative danger of enormous social upheavals of unforeseeable dimensions, their potential for joint action, are, in my opinion, in a better position than those of any other region to tackle this problem directly. Many of their leaders have already set forth the agenda concerning possible solutions to the foreign debt problem. This is the first step in a long and dangerous struggle.

It is inconceivable that the debtor countries in this hemisphere will not (sooner or later) form a cartel—even as the creditor countries themselves are closely joined together in the International Monetary Fund and the Paris Club. A club, cartel, committee, group—whatever you want to call it—is inevitable. Acting on their own, these states cannot achieve any kind of lasting solution for their problems; all they can hope to produce are palliative formulas that will mitigate the present difficulties: a brief grace period on the repayment of capital or a small reduction in the interest rate.

As I've already said, the problem no longer concerns just the repayment of the original sum. Even if a 4-, 6-, 8-, or 10-year grace period were granted, the problem would still grow worse and worse. The current renegotiations will solve absolutely nothing. The problem resides in the enormous amounts of interest that must be paid each year, religiously and punctually, accompanied by superimposed political and economic measures that cannot be enforced. These include: exaggerated, unrealistic goals to reduce inflation; the immediate reduction of budgetary deficits; the limitation of social expenditures in countries riddled with problems in education, health care, nutrition, housing, unemployment, etc.; and other such measures demanded by the International Monetary Fund. These become impossible to apply when the country is also forced to pay the enormous sums in unfair interest charged on its debt. The little people don't understand this. There is no message for them but the song of fruitless sacrifice: they've been promised a lot of things for a very long time, and they clearly see that things are getting worse and worse. They don't understand the technical aspects at all. They mean nothing to people who can't find work or who see their wages shrinking while products grow more and more expensive. "You can't fool all of the people all of the time."

Paradoxically, this crisis is providing Latin America and the other Third World countries with their first real opportunity to receive due consideration of their demands. We have spent dozens of years in the United Nations, in the Movement of Non-Aligned Countries, in all the other international organizations, demanding a fairer economic order, and requesting better prices for our products, loans, and resources for development. It wasn't long ago when, speaking on behalf of the Movement of Non-Aligned Countries, following its Sixth Summit Conference, I stated that the Third World needs no less than $300 billion in developmental assistance during this decade. It isn't just a matter of getting down on our knees and imploring the industrialized nations to give us the funds or to assign us a modest 0.7% of their combined gross national products—a commitment only a few of these states have made. Now, when they demand that the Latin American countries pay to them $400 billion over 10 years, the decision-making has passed to us. We have the power simply to declare that we won't accept this plunder, that we will not pay. They can't even threaten us with the suspension of future loans. Well used, that $400 billion could finance Latin America's development over the next 10 years or longer. Every country, in effect, could lend itself what it's paying in interest.

If the industrialized countries behave rationally, not only will they benefit from our increased exports, but their banks will also benefit. A formula such as the one I suggested would guarantee these institutions the availability of credits, from which they could make new loans and investments. This, when you get down to it, is their purpose in international finance. If the New International Economic Order is really achieved, such loans could be received and repaid on a solid fiscal basis, without risk to either party.

When the Organization of Petroleum Exporting Countries (OPEC) systematically raised the price of oil from approximately $2.50 to $30 a barrel, the industrialized countries—Europe, the United States, Japan, and others—began paying billions in added energy costs, totalling more than $1 trillion extra in just the last decade. This was much more than the entire accumulated foreign debt of the Third World—with interest—and it didn't ruin their economies or even affect their enormous military expenditures. Ninety percent of this money ended up in the banks of the same countries from which it had originated, reinvested by the oil states themselves. They also collected the extra cash that the non-oil-producing Third World countries were forced to spend on oil imports. The prices of exports soared. Many western companies, particularly arms manufacturers, were able to make fabulous deals, thanks to the new purchasing power of their oil-producing clients. The West was also forced to adopt scores of measures to save fuel, to finance the search for new technological innovations, and to explore new and old sources of energy. Waste was considerably reduced. Only the non-oil-producing countries of the Third World suffered irretrievably from this catastrophe, and were subjected to even more unequal terms of trade.

The cancellation of the Third World's foreign debt would be fair and economically beneficial for all countries, and much less costly in the long run than the West's meek submission to the oil exporters' demands.

The New International Economic Order will mean fairer trade relations for Third World countries; it will also mean that the rich, industrialized powers will have to stop wasting so much of the world's vital resources on arms. No one has the right to pay starvation wages for cocoa, tea, coffee, cashew nuts, peanuts, coconuts, fibers that are gathered leaf by leaf and grain by grain, minerals, or other raw materials just so they can manufacture aircraft carriers, battleships, strategic missiles, nuclear submarines, and "Star Wars" weapons. Those resources should be invested in the war on hunger, here on earth.

If the Latin American and Third World countries take a firm, united stand, they will, for the first time, have a real opportunity to achieve those goals, beginning with the question of the foreign debt. But if a total lack of understanding should force them to make a unilateral decision to default, they could not be threatened with a total suspension of trade. The rest of the world simply could not survive without their goods. They can't do without our fuel and other raw materials, and they certainly would not be happy without our coffee, tea, cocoa, shrimp, lobsters, and other tropical delights.

It is absolutely impossible for them to blockade the Third World economically or to take over our countries because of the debt, as they did in Haiti, the Dominican Republic, and elsewhere during the first few decades of this century. And they no longer have the will or the means to divide up the world again to ensure their supplies of raw materials and markets, as they did on other continents in earlier eras.

The new Latin American leaders have a tremendous responsibility. I repeat: if the problem of the debt isn't solved, if efforts are made to repay it at whatever cost, if the disastrous formulas of the International Monetary Fund are instituted, great social upheavals will occur.

I see little danger of a return to the pattern of right-wing, repressive, fascist *coups*, although some may take place in certain countries on an isolated basis. Rather, I think it is possible that, when great social upheavals occur, leaders imbued with a patriotic spirit and a realistic sense of the situation, men who are ready to promote social changes along with the people, will surely arise from among the military.

We have already seen much less critical circumstances produce such figures such as Torrijos in Panamá and Alvarado in Perú who held high the banners of nationalism and social reform.

The struggle for the solution to the foreign debt problem, for the promotion of fair economic relations between the Third World countries and the industrialized world, is so essential for the survival and future of the Latin American peoples that it would undoubtedly be supported by all social strata, generating great internal unity in their countries. It would also strengthen the solidarity between the Latin American nations, and would certainly receive the unhesitating, enthusiastic, determined support of all the developing countries in Asia and Africa. I have no doubt that many of the industrialized countries would also support these demands. Nor do I doubt that the most constructive solution lies in political dialogue and negotiation, which would promote agreement in an orderly manner. If this is not done, desperate situations will doubtless force a group of countries to take unilateral measures. This isn't desirable, but if it occurs, I am sure that the other countries in Latin America and the rest of the Third World would join them.

ELLIOT: You have stated that you see little danger of new dictators emerging in Latin America, despite the fact that many of these countries have had long periods of one-person rule. Why?

CASTRO: The people in several Latin American countries are now emerging from a veritable inferno. Their main concern is to leave that inferno behind. They have chosen the paths that provide the quickest, easiest, surest way out of that inferno.

The pattern of repressive military *coups* has already been tried *ad nauseam*, and the military are now extricating themselves from public administration in those countries, because they can't deal with the situation. The only one left is Pinochet, and he's ever more isolated, both at home and abroad—a kind of Somoza South, building up the pressure in the boiler that is Chile. If he stays too long, Chile may explode with such force that it will make Nicaragua look like a church meeting. Under normal situations countries such as Bolivia, with a tenth of the problems that have occurred there in recent times, would have already had a dozen military *coups* were it not for the sword of Damocles hanging over it.

DYMALLY: Still, Latin America's history suggests the real possibility of military intervention in an unstable political and social environment.

CASTRO: I don't really think so, and I'll tell you why. This military option was used to confront earlier crises that were only a pale reflection of the present situation. Starting with Brazil, more than 20 years ago; then in Chile; then in Uruguay; and still later in Argentina. These strong-arm military regimes caused tens of thousands of people to simply disappear; tens of thousands more were murdered, tortured, or forced into exile. Never before, except perhaps in Nazi Germany, had such horrible repressive methods been used. The people do not forget.

ELLIOT: However, if the centrist governments fall, could not the people democratically elect a right-wing regime?

CASTRO: As a rule, in any crisis situation the party in power loses support rapidly, and the people move toward the opposition; whenever you have a government of the left or of the right, conservative or liberal (though these words no longer imply any great differences), people in stable societies shift to the opposition party because they blame the party in power for the problems which exist.

If the present economic and social climate in Latin America continues to deteriorate, I don't believe that future political developments will take place through an idyllic, constitutional, or political process. Perhaps I'm being too pessimistic—the situation in Venezuela and Ecuador isn't as bad as say, that of Bolivia. Venezuela might survive, battered but still functioning. One can't always generalize about such things when so many different countries are involved. But there is no doubt that the debt crisis has already begun to affect all governments, to a greater or lesser degree. None can be excluded from consideration, none will wholly escape the *götterdammerung*.

Still, I believe that, if a solution isn't found soon, South America is going to explode. I am utterly convinced of this. The old panaceas have already been tried; methods used throughout history have already been exhausted. The present crisis is more serious, deeper, and more generalized than ever before. The military regimes are returning to their barracks; they cannot manage their countries, and they have left their democratic replacements a fearsome legacy. Now, the civilians have the responsibility of finding solutions.

If you ask me—as one journalist recently did—"As a revolutionary, aren't you glad that this is happening?," I will give you an honest reply. Right now, there is something more important than social change, and that is our countries' independence. The situation has brought the Third World countries to such a state of dependence, exploitation, extortion, and abuse that independence and the struggle for the New International Economic Order have become the main issues for Latin America and the other underdeveloped countries. Social changes alone are not the solution. Such changes may bring about greater justice, may speed development, may make the efforts and sacrifices of all more equitable, more humane, even more bearable. Cuba has made some of these changes and is satisfied that it has done so, but the considerable progress that Cuba has made in economic and social development wasn't due to the changes alone. Within our sphere, we have—to some extent—achieved a New International Economic Order in our own relations with the other socialist countries. Eighty-five percent of our trade is with countries of the socialist community, and, while the terms aren't the same with all of them (they have different levels of development and resources), our relations are based on truly fair principles of cooperation and trade.

For example, we seem to have overcome, in our trade relations with the Soviet Union and the other developed socialist countries, the tragic imbalance in terms that has historically plagued the relations between the Third World and the developed capitalist powers. We receive fair prices for the products we export, prices that are protected by fixed agreements that prevent deterioration in the terms of trade—the phenomenon by which the Third World countries have traditionally been victimized. Consequently, having seen a good example at work in Cuba, we consider the struggle for the New International Economic Order—which was discussed and agreed to at the United Nations ten years ago, largely thanks to México's initiative—to be essential in the short term. Marx himself always considered economic development to be a premise for socialism. Experience and chance forced a number of countries, Cuba among them, to take the socialist road of development. People should decide for themselves what they want to do. I am absolutely convinced that the peoples of the Third World, despite a great variety of systems of government, different degrees of development and the most diverse forms of political and religious beliefs, must place economic development as their most important current task, a vital priority on which all can unite in a common struggle.

We must get to the bottom of the problems that have created underdevelopment, that have adversely affected our countries' development, and that are widening the gap between the industrialized countries and the countries of the Third World. It has often been said that the gap should and must be closed, but it continues to widen, and is now, in fact, wider than ever before.

Some industrialized countries have reached production figures of $15,000 per person. Compare that with Africa's per capita production figure of barely a few hundred dollars a year, or with the figure for Latin America. The ratio was 10 to 1 some time ago, but now it has reached 15, 20, 30, 40, or (in some cases) 50 to 1. The gap between the industrialized world and the underdeveloped world is widening at an ever-increasing rate.

The per capita income gap is also widening. Far from making progress, we are regressing; instead of developing, we are becoming more underdeveloped. When the differences between us and the industrialized countries are increasing, when we are falling further behind with each passing day—even if a mathematical index says that we have grown by 2% to 3%—there is no doubt our world is obviously becoming progressively poorer in comparison to the developed world. The situation is even worse because, while the population in the industrialized countries is growing annually by a mere 0.6%, 0.7%, or 0.8%, the population in the Third World is growing by 2% to 3%. By the end of the century, 80% of the world's population will be living in the Third World. This is why I say that a new system of international economic relations, one which will really make development possible, is of paramount importance.

It follows, then, that if the New International Economic Order isn't promulgated, the terrible problems affecting our countries won't be solved simply through social changes. I repeat: even in a poor country, gradual social change can bring about more equal distribution of goods and can solve important social problems, both by promoting respect for human life, and by reducing injustice and inequality that may exist. I consider the struggle for the New Internatinal Economic Order to be the most important action Latin America and the Third World countries can now take, because it can lead to the creation of conditions needed for our real independence and our real sovereignty—and even the right (and possibility) to carry out significant social changes.

There is one essential point I must make: the cancellation of Latin America's foreign debt would not in itself solve all of our problems; it would merely offer us a few years' respite.

There are several countries in Latin America (Bolivia, for example) where the problems have become so serious that cancelling their debts wouldn't have any impact. They might be able to count on an additional $200 or $270 million, but their economic problems have reached such proportions that $270 million wouldn't even give them a "breather." A pound of tin which costs Bolivia $16 to produce can only be sold (at current world market prices) for $5 a pound. This is not unusual, unfortunately.

Of course, some countries are in better shape and would find cancellation of their debts a godsend; these nations include: Argentina, Uruguay, Brazil, Venezuela, Colombia, Ecuador, Perú, and México.

Ultimately, however, there can be no final solution for our problems so long as trade terms continue to deteriorate; so long as the industrialized capitalist powers continue to impose protectionist policies; so long as they continue to dump subsidized products in order to grab markets and depress the prices of those exports on which many Third World countries rely; so long as monetary policies are imposed on us which enable a powerful industrial country to determine what interest will be paid; so long as the capital needed for our development is drained away; and so long as models and methods such as the ones recommended by the Chicago School are imposed on us against our will. Not long ago, in a note to the Government of the United States, the Andean Pact countries expressed their deep concern over the drastic unilateral reductions that are being made in the amount of sugar which they can legally sell to the U.S. The United States—which in 1981 was still importing 5 million tons of sugar—reduced such imports to 2.7 million tons in 1984, and has promised to cut them even further to 1.7 million tons. The affected countries have described the situation as intolerable. These protectionist measures by the United States will reduce Latin

America's revenues by hundreds of millions of dollars, and will create surpluses that will further depress world market prices.

While Batista was in power, Cuba could sell over 3 million tons of sugar annually to the U.S. Then we were suddenly cut off and our quota was parceled out among other countries in this hemisphere. The pretext used by the American government was the necessity to crush the Cuban Revolution. Now, with the Latin debt approaching $360 billion, what pretext will the United States use?

Thus, if we don't consider these problems as a whole, we will obtain only a temporary respite, which will undoubtedly benefit a few countries, but will not address the basic causes of the situation. Now is the time to begin this struggle. Such a serious crisis is forming that the Third World countries are being forced to think, to unite, to seek solutions, regardless of their political stands or ideologies, as a matter of survival.

However, I do believe that Latin America has the means in hand to wage this economic war. We are not without weapons, the chief of which is simply our refusal to continue down the primrose path laid out for us by the U.S. and others. To solve the problem of the debt, the developing states in Asia and Africa must be willing to join with those of us in Latin America in the struggle. The debt must be cancelled. Mathematically, it is quite impossible to pay.

Our battle no longer involves just the original debt, but also the interest that is being paid on it. I base my view on 4 hypotheses which I have developed, all derived from the assumption that the debt itself won't increase.

First: that a 10-year grace period be granted for repaying the original debt; that interest will continue to be paid during this period, as it has so far; and that 10 years will be allowed for its amortization at an interest rate not exceeding 10%. Latin America would have to pay $400 billion during the first 10 years and an additional $558 billion in the next 10. In 20 years, Latin America would have transferred some $958 billion to its creditors. Nearly a trillion dollars would be drained from these countries, in spite of their enormous social and economic problems, and the potential development they would be forced to forego. Is this really possible? I say no. Any government which tried to squeeze this money from its long-suffering people would soon find itself overturned.

Second: that we limit payment of the debt to a maximum of 20% of the value of each country's exports, and that interest rates still don't exceed 10% annually. The Latin American exports now approach in aggregate some $100 billion per year. We can presume that no more than $20 billion of this will be available annually to repay the debt. Simple mathematics tell us that we would pay some $400 billion plus over a 20-year period. At the end of that span, we would still have an outstanding debt of $1,161,850 trillion—that is, our debt would be triple what it is today.

Third: that a 10-year grace period be granted, including the interest; an additional 10 years be granted for its amortization; and the interest still doesn't exceed 10% in any given year. Even with a 10-year respite, $1,447,310 million would still be owed 2 decades later.

Fourth: that the interest rate be lowered to 6%; that a 10-year grace period be granted, including interest; and that an additional 10 years are allowed in which to repay the debt. This would certainly be the kindest of the 4 formulas. However, 20 years later, $857,471 billion would still be owed.

These 4 hypotheses assume the best of all possible scenarios—that is, that the debt would not grow and that the interest rates would not exceed 10%. They demonstrate conclusively that the debt and its interest simply cannot be paid, under any foreseeable circumstances.

It can't be done from a practical viewpoint—our economies couldn't survive it—and it will never solve our development problems. The debt is an economic and a political impossibility. It is also a moral impossibility. The immense sacrifices that would have to be demanded of the people, and the blood that would have to be shed to force them to pay, is completely unjustifiable, according to any ethical system of which I am aware. The debt has already taken its first toll in the Dominican Republic, where dozens of poor people were killed. Any attempt to pay the debt under the present social, economic, and political circumstances in Latin America would cost our suffering and impoverished nations rivers of blood, if it could be done. The people are not to blame for their own under-development or for a debt which was incurred by irresponsible governments. Our countries are not to blame for having been colonies, neocolonies, banana republics, or coffee, mining, or oil republics, whose traditional role was to provide low-cost raw materials, exotic products, and fuel for the industrialized nations.

Economic historians tell us that the fabulous amounts of gold and silver that were extracted from the entrails of our nations over the centuries, thanks to our peoples' sweat and blood, helped finance the development of the industrialized world, the very same creditors who are now demanding repayment of the debt. The amount wrenched away from our peoples in just the last few decades through unequal terms of trade, high interest rates, protectionism, dumping, monetary manipulations, and the flight of capital, is much greater than the total amount of the debt. The riches of which we have been deprived through the imposition of economic dependence and underdevelopment cannot even be estimated, let alone measured. By right, we should be the creditors of the rich and industrialized western world, both morally and materially.

The Federal Republic of Germany has been paying Israel cash compensation for the Nazis' genocide against the Jews. Who is compensating us for the deliberate destruction of our peoples' lives and riches over the past four centuries?

The Latin American debt is unpayable and should be cancelled. It has been said that failure to pay the debt would destabilize and sink the international financial system. This isn't necessarily so. I suggest that the industrialized creditor countries can and should make themselves responsible for the debts to their own banks.

Historically, the public debt of the industrialized countries has increased with each passing decade—they have managed the problem by assuming responsibility for payment of the interest on the debt. The principal is rarely reduced. The U.S. public debt reached $1 trillion in 1981; from 1981 to 1984, just 3 years, it increased by another $650 billion; and it will soon exceed $2 trillion. However, the Reagan administration doesn't seem much concerned. Government officials stress the inherent strength of the economy even though it is growing at a rate of only 5% annually. According to official government pronouncements, the increase in the American debt has neither ruined the economy nor impeded its growth, nor has it hampered the optimism with which some U.S. economists talk about the future economic growth of their country. If the United States and the other industrialized powers were to make themselves responsible to their private banks for the debts of Latin America and the Third World, this would undoubtedly add an unknown amount to their national debt.

Where could they find the resources to pay the interest on their increased debts without hurting their economies? That's easy: from military expenditures—not all military expenditures, just a small percentage of them: say 10% or, if interest rates go up again, a maximum of 12%.

With a modest reduction in military expenditures, the industrialized powers could make themselves responsible to their own banks for the foreign debts of the Latin American and other Third World countries—and military spending would still be high enough in the world to be a real cause for concern.

Military spending throughout the world now amounts to a million trillion dollars. The arms race is both absurd and unacceptable in a world in which there are more than 100 underdeveloped countries and billions of people who lack food, health care, housing, and education. If it doesn't end soon, uncontrolled military spending will ultimately unleash a nuclear catastrophe, which would be far more dangerous than the slow economic catastrophe from which a large part of mankind is suffering. The former would end this philosophical discussion—and all others—permanently.

It would be very sensible and wise if a reduction in military spending were associated with the beginning of a solution to the world's economic problems. Many economists have stated that, by diverting just a fraction of the money now being spent for arms, the poverty that besets the Third World could be eradicated forever. The dangers of increased military spending was the subject of a meeting held several years ago in New Delhi, in which such international figures as Gandhi, Nyerere, Alfonsín, de la Madrid, Papandreou, and Palme participated.

By issuing 10-year Treasury notes and bonds, the United States could make itself responsible to its own creditor banks for all the loans made to Latin America and Third World countries. This wouldn't affect its citizens' current tax burdens. The banks would recover the capital they had invested, U.S. export companies would increase their exports, and U.S. investors abroad would increase their profits. More importantly, such a solution would create jobs in all of the industrialzed countries; their industries would see a large increase in utilized plant capacity, and international trade would increase.

Remember, the main problem confronting the industrialzed countries isn't their cumulated debt domestic or foreign. It is the scourge of unemployment, which has steadily increased in most of the western nations over the past decade, with the figures approximating 3 million in Britain (despite its new oil resources); 2.6 million in the Federal Republic of Germany (a postwar record); 3 million in France; 2.8 million in Spain; and so on. Even in the United states unemployment figures are at levels which would have been politically unacceptable 10 or 15 years ago.

Solving the problem of the underdeveloped world's foreign debt would be a significant step toward ending the present internatinal economic crisis, which is far from over, despite the optimistic forecasts made by some western experts. The economy of the European Economic Community grew by a mere 2.4% in 1984; better results are not expected soon. According to very recent data, the U.S. economy also experienced significantly slower growth during the first quarter of this year.

Reducing the Third World's foreign debt would doubtless provide relief for many of these countries. Within a few years, however, many of the short-term benefits resulting from this policy would vanish, so long as the West continues its unequal trade terms, protectionist measures, dumping, unfair monetary policies, excessive interest on loans, and similar practices. If these aren't eliminated—that is, if a New International Economic Order isn't firmly established—the situation will remain in the long term on much the same level, or even worsen.

ELLIOT: Don't citizens lose confidence in a government that can't pay its debts or manage its economy?

CASTRO: People often lose confidence in such governments, but it isn't always right to do so; sometimes their leaders' replacements find themselves in equally difficult situations. Is it right to blame sincere men for a crisis not of their making? In many cases, the leaders of the debtor nations were seriously trying to find a quick way out of their countries' perpetual cycles of poverty, a cycle which directly resulted from a system of domination and exploitation that had been imposed on the underdeveloped world. The world economic crisis has affected precisely those who can afford it the least. The problem has been slowly developing over the last few decades; the severity of its consequences have depended both on each country's economic resources and also on the greater or lesser efficiency with which that country has defended itself against or tried to overcome the crisis, with widely varying results. Undoubtedly, the policies followed in Chile, Argentina, and Uruguay—the official policies of the military regimes—have had terrible consequences.

For example, in the last year of Allende's administration, Chile was importing $100 million worth of meat annually. Within a few months after the *coup*, however, Chile was exporting meat. How? From a series of events, including: the disappearance of thousands of opponents of the regime; massive layoffs of Chile's civil servants; a drastic cutback in social services; the wholesale firing of factory workers; severe wage cuts; and the substantial reduction of the people's standard of living. Within a year, many people who previously ate meat could no longer afford it, and so Pinochet was able to begin exporting it.

This wasn't the only thing Pinochet did. He presented himself as a champion of western principles, western values, capitalism, and free enterprise; as a result, American economic advisers, economic specialists, and professors of the Chicago School immediately appeared to show him how western interests (the interests of capitalism) really had to be defended. They expounded the theory that, if he wanted to have efficient industry, he would have to open the doors to foreign competition and place Chilean industries in competition with European, American, and Japanese industries and those of such countries as South Korea, Taiwan, and Singapore, where the big transnationals had taken their technologies and imposed their discipline—for which, of course, they also needed authoritarian regimes based on force. A principle that has been accepted as axiomatic for any developing country for many years—that the nascent industries of the developing countries have to be protected against the competition of countries with more resources, more technology, and more development—was abandoned. As a result, Chile's industry was destroyed, the number of unemployed increased substantially, and the national debt skyrocketed.

In Chile, the most sophisticated economic principles of the Chicago School resulted in an increase in the $4 billion foreign debt under Allende to $23 billion under Pinochet. Unemployment reached a record high for Latin America: 18.6% of the work force. These figures do not take into consideration the large number of underemployed, who work fewer hours than they desire in subsistence labor.

The same economic policies applied by the military dictatorship in Chile were also used in Argentina and Uruguay. You can imagine what happened when Argentina's automobile, truck, and tractor industries, which produce very high-quality vehicles—we should know, since we use Argentine vehicles in Cuba—were placed in direct competition with the Japanese truck and automobile industries, which have highly automated plants that employ robots in many operations and use Japanese steel made with high-technology, high-productivity industrial processes. Argentina's highly skilled workers could not possibly vie with Japan's much cheaper industrial machines.

I asked an emissary of the party that won the election in Uruguay what the military government had done there. He cited the case of a plant that produced hair curlers or something like that; when the same—but cheaper—South Korean articles appeared, the Uruguayan industry was destroyed. The same economic formula was applied in all of these countries, with equally dismal results. The situation was made worse in Chile, Argentina, and Uruguay, through the overt use of military force. You can appreciate the disastrous consequences of those political and economic measures.

The ironic paradox is that the United States, the most industrialized country in the world, employs all kinds of tariffs and other hidden taxes to jealously protect not only its industries (which are now far from competitive in many areas), but also its agricultural products, such as beet sugar and even corn syrup, for sweetening soft drinks. Yet, these American professors continue to preach the benefits of eliminating our trade barriers to make our industries competitive. Benefits to whom?

I have little hard information about Brazil, about what the military men did there economically, and how they did it—which formula they used to increase its debts so rapidly. I do have the impression, however, that Brazil didn't follow the exact same policies as Chile, Argentina, or Uruguay—that it may have protected its national industries more cannily against foreign competition—that it allowed the transnationals (who were attracted by the cheap labor) to invest in large industrial plants, offering them all the advantages, guarantees, and securities that a strong-arm regime could.

ELLIOT: How would you assess the long-term effects of the United States' economic boycott on Cuba? How long can Cuba survive without U.S. trade?

CASTRO: Clearly, it has cost us billions of dollars. In transportation alone, to cite but one example, if you have to import materials all the way from Japan or Europe, when you could have purchased them in the United States, a place 10 or 20 times closer, you find yourself spending several times as much on transportation. You may also have to pay higher prices, for the goods themselves, because the trader knows you have no alternative but to buy that merchandise in that country. If you calculate the damage done by America to Cuba by depriving her of her sugar quota, and from the price differential between what we would have received from the United States under previously existing agreements and the prices at which we now have to sell our sugar in Japan and other countries, it's a staggering amount of money.

If you further add the damage caused to our economy by cutting us off from supplies of spare parts for equipment based on U.S. technology, you can see that the damage was considerable.

Some of your government's actions were particularly difficult for me to understand, because they directly harmed innocent human beings. When you can't buy medical equipment made only in the United States, or import a particular medication that is needed to save a life, the consequences of the blockade cease to be just economic—they take on a human dimension. If a citizen of the U.S. had been a victim of such draconian measures, he could have sued or filed a complaint, claiming that material compensation was owed him. India has filed similar claims for the deaths of thousands of people maimed by leaking gas from a pesticide plant owned by a U.S. company. We have no such recourse. Still, leaving aside such considerations, the American blockade has cost our economy billions of dollars, perhaps as much as $10 billion. But, we've held out for 25 years, and we can hold out for another 25 years, or even 100 years. We've been forced to work harder, to be more austere, leaner, efficient. In other words, from necessity, we have developed certain virtues that are of enormous value to a developing country. We have struggled hard to find viable economic alternatives, to "make do," so to speak, and we have found them. We have turned what I consider to be U.S. economic aggression into a motivating force for our entire population. Ironically, the blockade has had almost exactly the opposite effect on us that the United States intended.

Obviously, we must trade with someone, so we have had to develop economic relations with other socialist and Third World countries, and have sought thereby to establish a New International Economic Order in the process. Consequently, Cuba was not a victim (as well it could have been) of unequal trade relations, interest spreads, an overvalued dollar, protectionist measures, or dumping of low quality products. Instead, we have established a solid foundation for our country's future economic and social development. We already know what we intend to do during the next 15 years in all fields of economic and social development, including industry, agriculture, housing, education, culture, sports, and medicine. Despite the blockade, there are some areas, such as public health and education, in which our achievements come very close to those of the United States, and we expect to surpass your country in selected fields in the not too distant future. That is, if we use our resources rationally to achieve sustained economic growth for the benefit of all the people, not just some. We certainly have no intentions of following Reagan's lead in cutting aid to the elderly, reducing old-age pensions, cutting medical programs for the sick, or reducing hospital and school appropriations. We won't sacrifice our social programs—as you do in the United States—for the sake of building aircraft carriers, MX missiles, and other weapons built solely to maim and kill. In Cuba, social assistance is a top-priority item: we increase such expenditures every year, as our economic performance improves. This is why Cuba is the only Latin American or Caribbean country which hasn't suffered much from the debt crisis. Only that portion of our trade (about 15%) which goes to western countries has been impacted in any way. The industrialized powers do charge high prices for their products, pay low prices for ours, and force us to pay high interest rates on our foreign debt in convertible currency, which is relatively modest. But 85% of our trade goes to the socialist community, and this is what has given us a solid foundation for future sustained growth. Thus, while the GNP and per capita products of the Latin American countries as a whole have dropped in the last five years, Cuba's economy grew by 24.8%, and its per capita production by 22.6%, during 1981-1984. This is noted in the annual economic reports of the United Nations Economic Commission for Latin America and the Caribbean, which contrasts Cuba's situation with that of the rest of Latin America.

The growth of the Cuban economy during the 1981-1984 period is higher—much higher—than all of the rest of the Latin American countries. In Argentina, the gross domestic product decreased by 6%; in Bolivia, by 16.1%; in Brazil, by 0.3%; in Chile, by 5.4%; in Perú, by 3.8%; and in Uruguay, by 13.9%. The list is quite long. I'm not even mentioning health and education, where our country is in first place among all the Third World nations, and ahead of several industrialized countries as well. We have no unemployment, begging, slums, prostitution, gambling, drugs, or alcoholism—problems that were endemic under Batista.

This is why I feel morally entitled to speak about the present economic crisis and the Latin American debt. I will not remain silent. We are secure precisely because we need depend very little on the western world, and specifically on economic relations with the United States. I wonder how many other countries in this part of the world can say the same.

DYMALLY: Let's speculate a little. Let's say the United States suddenly decides to lift its embargo. What effect would this have on the Cuban economy?

CASTRO: I believe that the United States has fewer and fewer things to offer Cuba. We export primarily sugar, but the United States has been systematically reducing its sugar imports, nearly eliminating the sugar quotas of many Latin American countries. So what are we going to sell to your country? The United States is drastically restricting its imports of Latin American steel. We export some steel for construction, but there's no market for it in the United States. The United States is imposing extremely low textile quotas on textile-exporting countries to protect its own internal production. The goods produced by our new textile mills, many of which have been modernized and expanded, could not be sold in the United States to any great degree.

As regards tourism, we have more demand than our hotel capacity. Certainly, lifting the blockade would be advantageous to both countries in the long run. I'm not saying we wouldn't derive some benefit, because that's just not true. Some goods that now have to be acquired from distant third parties could be obtained directly from the United States, thereby lowering freight costs and providing much speedier delivery. We would obviously want to purchase certain medical equipment or certain pharmaceutical products, or things of that sort. But there would not be much. It would be inconceivable, for example, for us to start importing Cadillacs and other such luxury items from the United States if our relations were somehow normalized. We can't pay for them and, we frankly don't need them—the U.S. can continue to export such things to other Latin American countries, to millionaires and greedy politicians who have the stolen money to buy them, even though their countries derive no benefit from such purchases (in fact, just the opposite).

Frankly speaking, renewed economic relations with the United States would not imply any major benefits for Cuba. If trade with the United States were suddenly opened tomorrow, and if we were miraculously allowed to export our Cuban products to the United States, we would have nothing to export, because everything we intend to produce in the next five years has already been sold to other markets. We would have to break agreements with our socialist friends in order to sell our goods to the United States, and the socialist countries pay much better prices and give us much better terms than does the United States.

Our citrus fruit, a large part of our sugar, much of our nickel, and most of our other products, all go to these markets. They pay us higher prices, and sell their products to us at lower prices, and also charge us much lower interest for credit, and automatically reschedule our debts at our request for 10, 15, or 20 years without interest. So what are we going to do? There's an old Cuban folk saying that says, "Don't swap a cow for a goat."

ELLIOT: When it comes to trade, does the United States treat western Europe differently than it does Latin America?

CASTRO: Unquestionably. The United States treats western Europe and Japan as equal trading partners, and their relations as those between friendly, industrialized, and fully developed countries. This is obvious from published statistics: the transnationals have investments valued at $625 billion, only $150 billion of which is in the Third World; of the $150 billion, 53% that is some $80 billion—is invested in Latin America and the Caribbean. This means that over 75% of these companies' investments are in the industrialized world. There are European companies in the United States and American firms in Europe. The same holds true in Japan and among the other industrialized countries. The phenomenon of unequal trade doesn't much occur there, even though the American economic system prevails in the western world, and it is the one that sets the standards and makes the rules. Of course, there are some difficulties among these nations: between the United States and Japan, between the United States and Europe, between Europe and Japan. Even so, they all somehow manage to get along fine, and between them have so many resources, so much productivity, that they can permit themselves the luxury of working fewer hours and a per capita income that is incomparably higher than that of the Third World. If the system were at all rational, hours could be reduced further and unemployment eliminated, but the system itself demands a reserve army of the unemployed. There is a growing difference between the per capita income of the industrialized countries and the per capita income of the developing countries.

On the other hand, the United States' relations with Latin America are uneven and unfair, as are the relations between other industrialized and Third World countries. I've already discussed at some length how the Latin American countries transfer huge resources to the industrialized countries every year. There's no comparison.

DYMALLY: Increasingly, the island ministates of the Caribbean are becoming dependent on the United States for economic assistance. Is this the best way to help these nations?

CASTRO: In today's world, the mere fact that a country is small, in both territory and population, constitutes a real obstacle for development, because most existing technology assumes a scale of production aimed at a much wider market.

For example, a 2000-kilowatt power plant consumes more fuel proportionately per unit of electric power produced than a 300,000-kilowatt thermoelectric power plant. Nuclear power plants are constructed with reactors at least 400 megawatts in size—smaller reactors just aren't built. Cuba has expressed the need to find a technical solution for this problem, which makes it impossible for many small oil-importing countries to use nuclear power. Often these states are unable to find economic sources of electric power from elsewhere simply because they are geographically isolated—this is particularly true in the Caribbean.

Europe and the Soviet Union have large power transmission lines to transfer electric power from east to west and vice versa every day from plants located all over Europe, so that each area receives what it needs during the hours of peak demand. When it is 8:00 A.M. in an eastern city, it could be 4:00 P.M. in a western city. This allows the plants to operate at full capacity. Some electricity flows even betweeen the socialist countries in Europe and those in the West. The United States has similar facilities, and even exchanges power with Canada; the same is true for gas and oil pipelines, roads, and railways linking all major continental states. Nothing like this is feasible among the small nations of the Caribbean.

When a country is physically isolated—even when the island is large, as in Cuba's case—it can't receive gas, oil, electricity, or solid or liquid cargoes of any kind through any overland transit. Everything must either be produced in the country itself or imported by ship. If the island is very small, its problems multiply. If you want to build a textile plant, for example, the minimum capacity required for a cost-effective scale of production is 25 million square meters of fabric. If you're dealing with a cement plant, you should build a plant that produces at least 300,000 tons a year—smaller ones aren't even made. The problems of economic development in the Caribbean states are both complex and very difficult just because they are small and isolated.

These countries need serious, creative solutions if they are to overcome their inherent limitations, and become anything other than havens for tourism, pleasure, and gambling, with nice coconut trees and exotic nooks to be enjoyed by privileged travelers from the industrialized world. Jamaica is somewhat larger and has a population of over 2 million; it can attain some kind of autonomous development. The same is true of Trinidad and Tobago. But most of the rest can't function without an economic community helping to support them all.

Western Europe could not survive if it were not for the European Economic Community. How can a group of small islands, which were colonies just a short time ago, survive and develop without some form of economic integration? Only on this basis can they achieve some degree of industrial development, taking into account the natural and human resources available on each of the islands, the group's potential market force, and their potential export to other areas. Most of these states speak the same language and have the same cultural background. An economic community is a prerequisite for and guarantee of the viability of their independence. The industrialized countries, including the United States, should open their trade doors to the products of these countries and of any other nations that need development. The so-called Caribbean Basin Initiative includes this idea on a limited basis, but the project as a whole is permeated by the idea that the transnationals will eventually take over these countries. The financial development of the Caribbean is somehow perceived solely as a matter of private business, the aid to be offered by U.S. investors. Rather than developing each state on a national basis, with local investments, the plan proposes the use of foreign entrepreneurs, with local cheap labor—the workers' wages being the only thing that would remain in the country. In exchange, these countries would be granted tariff and tax exemptions of all sorts, but even chewing gum and soft drinks would still have to come from the United States. It's the same old story of banana republics and Big Brother. But this kind of program will do nothing to integrate the Caribbean countries or unite them. Rather, it will splinter them, forcing them to compete with one another, and facilitate their manipulation by external powers. We simply can't agree with that approach.

In Puerto Rico—which was once hailed as a model of this type of development—some $20 billion was invested in the economy, largely in various polluting industries. Twenty years later, a very large number of people remain unemployed, and almost half of the population must rely on food stamps to subsist.

The Eastern Caribbean islands—and many other regions of the world, as well—need large-scale international cooperation for their development. They can't survive on their own resources. What is required is the kind of economic and social development that promotes the people's welfare—not the profits and business interests of the transnationals, which are the only groups ultimately to be served by the cheap market facilities now being offered to them. Foreign cooperation, of course, remains essential.

DYMALLY: Obviously you regard America as the corrupting Godfather of the western Hemisphere. Suppose the United States were to cancel the Latin American debt and simultaneously provide a substantial increase in foreign assistance. Would this immediately improve United States-Cuban relations?

CASTRO: Let me answer your question in this way. The debt should be cancelled, not for any immediate political benefits which might accrue to the U.S., but because such cancellation would benefit economically both the United States and every other country in the world. This would help overcome the present crisis, a financial problem which has begun affecting even the United States's rather robust economy. During the last four years, the Reagan administration has used its monetaristic policies and huge economic power to skillfully impose a financial lock on the rest of the world, forcing not only the Third World countries—who were helpless—but also its Spanish, French, Italian, English, West German, and Japanese allies to accept it. Through its Federal Reserve Bank, the United States decides how much money should circulate in the world's markets, and what the interest rates should be to exclusively solve its own problems of inflation, unemployment, and economic stagnation.

Many of America's economic ills derive directly from a runaway arms race. Economists now know that the high military expenditures of the Vietnam war were one of the main causes of the huge inflation that hit the world economy then. The United States spent hundreds of billions of dollars without raising taxes, because the war was so unpopular that the people would have balked at any new levies.

Today, the United States is spending more than it did on the Vietnam war—and it is promoting rearmament without raising the funds to support it. Reagan has tried to finance his new army and navy partly by cutting back on public expenditures—assistance to senior citizens, the sick, and the schools. But monies saved by these cuts haven't been nearly enough, because military spending has grown enormously: from $135 billion in 1980 to $277 billion in 1985 to $314 billion in 1986. There's not enough left for developing industrial technology or for making industry more efficient and productive. Instead, huge sums are allocated for very expensive equipment that contributes absolutely nothing to the economy. That's a fact.

The Reagan administration has miraculously and simultaneously managed to push an arms race without a tax increase, a reduction in inflation, an increase in production, and a decrease in unemployment. It's as if he had an Aladdin's lamp or the wild ass's skin of Balzac's novel. But you could only ask the lamp for 3 wishes, and Reagan has asked for these and more. Magic lamps don't work forever, and one usually pays a high (and sometimes hidden) price for those "free" gifts. Someday the members of the brain trust that gave Reagan this magic formula will have to be found and given citations for the "Order of Machiavelli." Certainly, they knew very clearly what they were doing, even if Reagan didn't. The United States now has far more battleships, aircraft carriers, bombers, nuclear submarines, cruise missiles, and arms of all sorts than they did before. This is how Reagan ran for re-election: bombs without pain.

But it makes you wonder. Money doesn't fall from the sky like rain; it has to come from somewhere. It makes you wonder how Reagan accomplished all this and how it was paid for. I think that's a question American citizens should be asking themselves— and what the future consequences will be. Consider this one small fact: the American public debt, which took 205 years to reach $1 trillion, increased by $650 billion in just 3 years under the Reagan administration (1981-1984). By the end of 1986, after 5 years of the Reagan administration, it will amount to more than $2 trillion.

The economists advising Reagan have managed to achieve in 5 years what it took all of his predecessors 205 years to do. In addition, his budget deficit, which he promised to eradicate, now exceeds $200 billion annually, and, at its present rate, should reach $300 billion a year by the end of his term. Last year's trade deficit exceeded $100 billion. Another Olympic record. This year, the trade deficit may top $150 billion.

I ask you: where is this money coming from? How can this economic "miracle," this American economic miracle, be explained? How has Reagan managed to turn water into wine? How did he work the miracle of multiplying the fish and the loaves? Based on Reagan's performance, perhaps we should consider founding a new church, with him as prophet, because what we are witnessing is nothing short of miraculous. There may be other miracles yet to come. Where does the money come from? From everybody, of course. One way or the other, the cash to support this house of cards comes from the Japanese, the Germans, the English, the Italians, the Spaniards, and all the other industrialized and Third World countries who have brought it to the United States. This is an unprecedented phenomenon.

In recent years foreigners have invested close to $200 billion in U.S. bonds—and that's only the bonds. It's possible to estimate the total amount of foreign deposits in the United States—which, as *The Washington Post* recently stated, is living far above its own production levels and is already the largest debtor nation in the world, owing more than all the Latin American countries put together—at roughly $600 billion, give or take a few billion.

Of course, I suspect that the United States, which has received overvalued dollars during the past decade, will try to pay its debts with devaluated dollars in the future. It will surely have a different policy as a debtor than as a creditor. It lent cheap dollars and is collecting expensive ones; it obtained loans and deposits in expensive dollars and will try to pay its debts with cheap ones.

I'd like to imagine what the consequences of all this will be on future inflation—and what impact this will have on the buying power of the U.S. dollar, how much inflation will amount to, and if the "wizards" advising Reagan know when this phenomenon will take place—for it will take place, unquestionably. What will be the consequences to the future American economy of spending $2 trillion in only 8 years for military purposes, instead of investing it in industrial, technological, and economic development? The only significant development has been registered by the arms industry, but weapons aren't goods that the population can consume. Rifles, bullets, bombs, bombers, battleships, and aircraft carriers increase neither the wealth nor the productive capacity of a country—and they certainly can't meet any of man's material or spiritual needs. You can't even fish with those boats; you can't do anything with them that's useful for human life, health, or the struggle against cancer and other diseases that kill so many United States citizens every year.

There are three diseases that kill the majority of American citizens: cancer, heart disease, and related circulatory problems. I don't have the exact figures, but, in a population of 240 million, you can estimate that over a million people die every year from these 3 causes. No war has ever killed so many Americans. If some of this money could be diverted to fighting these diseases—there is never enough money for medical research—the lives of all the people in the world would be bettered.

That $2 trillion doesn't produce an aspirin; it doesn't cure a single headache. Someday, Americans will regret the waste of their industrial facilities, and the fact that they could have been more efficient, and more productive; they'll be sorry that the environment has become irreversibly polluted; they'll feel the lack of hospitals, recreation facilities, schools, homes for the elderly, and low-cost housing.

The conservatives are going to say, "If disarmament is the only option, we'll have nothing to do with it." But there is another alternative: to rid ourselves of prejudice, lies, and anachronistic myths; to eliminate the far-fetched dream of sweeping other ideologies and social systems off the face of the earth; to stop attributing the craziest, most absurd intentions to one's adversaries; and to really talk with the Soviets and work out a lasting peace for all mankind. After all, the Soviets understand these realities even better than do the people of the United States: they have experienced the tragedy of war in a way you will never understand, and they have a greater concern for, and feeling of responsibility toward, the need for averting a nuclear conflict, something which would be utterly catastrophic and—in all likelihood—suicidal for the human race.

A socialist can better understand—is better prepared to understand, from a theoretical point of view—the folly of spending huge sums of money on weapons when those same resources could be used to meet the pressing problems of human society. All socialist states know what can and should be done with those resources, both at home and abroad. The poverty and disasters that plague our planet are obvious. Why not opt for a serious, sincere effort to seek peace and cooperation among all countries, based on full respect for the sovereignty and the social systems that these people have chosen for themselves?

The ultimate consequences of these enormous arms expenditures on the economy of the United States are yet to be seen; that they will impact inflation and the country's economic development is inevitable. No matter how rich in natural resources a country may be, it can't squander its wealth and that of others with total impunity. I think it's high time for all Americans to reflect on this harsh economic reality.

Ronald Reagan was re-elected in November, 1984 under the bewitching influence of his economic "miracles"; the impact on November, 1988 is yet to be seen. Some things can already be seen. The Senate Appropriations Committee has adopted a resolution calling for drastic trade restrictions against Japan—tantamount to declaration of a trade war against Japan. Similar measures have been discussed against other countries. The United States had a 1984 trade deficit with Japan of some $37 billion, an amount that is expected to reach $50 billion or more this year. The Japanese aren't producing battleships, MX missiles, B-1 bombers, or Trident submarines; they're investing their hard-earned money in industry and development, just as they've done consistently over the last 30 years, since World War II. This is why they have such modern, automated industrial, electronic, chemical, and steel industries. Moreover, they're more austere, better organized, and more disciplined than most Americans. So it's only logical that they can compete successfully with the U.S. in that country's own domestic markets. The United States seems ready to set quotas and adopt other measures against the free market and free enterprise, demanding an equal share of the Japanese market, and undertaking a series of initiatives that directly contradict what it claims as its own economic philosophy.

There are people in the United States—thousands of people well versed in economic matters—who agonize about the consequences of America's tremendous arms expenditures without commensurate revenues. It is a problem that should be debated in the House, in the Senate, and by the academic community, to see if these so-called "miracles" can be explained. What is clear in Latin America is that economies have declined. Nor have we seen any growth in much of the Third World. Europe's economy has grown minimally, while unemployment there has increased significantly. The United States has reduced unemployment—from nearly 11% to approximately 7%—but in England, the number of unemployed has risen to 3 million; in France, to 3 million; in Spain, to 2.8 million; and, in the Federal Republic of Germany, to a postwar record of 2.6 million. And unemployment is still growing. These things begin to explain the "miracle." In the last quarter of 1984, the United States Treasury—as reported by official U.S. statistics—borrowed $72 billion, a record figure. The present administration and its economic advisers have produced "miracles," all right, with stupendous increases in budget deficits, trade deficits, foreign indebtedness, and the growth of the public debt. You're all living on borrowed time.

What are the long-term consequences of this policy? This is a question that American citizens must ask themselves. We too have the right to ask. Clearly, the Third World will be profoundly affected by the answer, in one way or the other. What is it all for? To improve people's lives, health, or security? No. If the United States had incurred these deficits just to develop its economy or to increase production, this might have been acceptable, even though such a realization at the expense of rest of the world might not have been very honest. If the money had been invested to increase your standard of living, one could say, "It isn't right to mortgage a nation for such a purpose." Certainly, we couldn't do that here. But still, at least you could feel that you'd created something. But you've done none of these. Instead, you've spent a fantastic sum of money on war materiel that will become totally obsolete and good only for scrap in no more than 10 or 15 years. That's my view of what's happening in the United States.

You asked me what my reaction would be if the United States were to cancel the debt and also offer increased assistance to Latin America. As I have already said, the cancellation of the debt itself would suffice. This may happen if the United States becomes convinced that there is no alternative, or if the Latin American countries unilaterally declare the debt cancelled, a more likely prospect. They could do this by common consent. If a policy of austerity followed, their own resources would suffice for development. No additional outside injections of funds would be necessary. It's more important, perhaps, to solve Latin America's other economic problems: to obtain fair prices for its goods (that is, to put an end to the growing deterioration of trade that now favors the industrialized countries); to end all protectionist measures; and to end the practice of dumping. If the Latin American countries had received in 1984 what they received in 1980 from their exports, they could have earned an additional $20 billion just from that. That's just one example.

Naturally, the Latin American countries will have to adopt effective measures to avoid the flight of foreign currency that has meant such serious monetary losses in the past. But, so long as the present monetaristic policies are in effect, so long as the dollar is overvalued, and so long as 12-13% interest rates are being paid, Latin Americans will endeavor to send their money to the United States. If these end, and if Latin America stops sending $70 billion to the industrialized world every year, including the interest on its huge debt, no massive injections of money would be needed for our development. Then, if you add to the cancellation of the debt a small percentage of the world's military expenditures, additional development loans could easily be made available—and repaid! I don't expect anything of the sort to happen, being the realist that I am, but if the United States were to spontaneously do what you say, then a real "miracle" would have taken place, and I would have to start meditating on that subject. Perhaps I would even consult several theologians and philosophers and rethink my positions on religion. I might even enter a monastery!

DYMALLY: If you had the power to impose your "New International Economic Order" on the world, what would it include and what would it do?

CASTRO: It's impossible for any one person to define or to even outline all the aspects of what should constitute a "New International Economic Order." Various ideas have been discussed at length in the United Nations; at the initiative of Algeria, México, and other countries, a set of proposals was adopted almost unanimously 10 years ago. It just hasn't been implemented. The industrialized western countries have blocked every attempt to have the issue raised again—irrefutable proof of the hypocrisy and scorn with which they treat us. I am a convinced and determined defender of these ideas, in which many of the finest minds of the Third World invested thousands of working hours.

I believe that certain principles are fundamental: the starting point is the fact that there are two economic worlds on this globe; an immensely rich, economically, industrially, technologically, and scientifically developed world; and sharing the same planet and sometimes the same space, a much poorer step-sister where 70% of the world's population now lives, and where, by the end of the century—15 years from now—80% will live, because the population of those countries is growing by 2%-3% a year.

The countries that comprise the Third World were colonies of the European powers in the not too distant past; the people of the United States recall that their country was once an English colony. The present industrialized countries—the former colonial powers and their more privileged colonies, such as the United States (where the African slave trade and slavery continued for almost a century after its independence)—now constitute the nuclei of industrial development in the western world. I believe these states are historically responsible for the rest of the world's underdevelopment, because, for centuries, they plundered those countries systematically.

It was the gold and silver extracted from the mines of Latin America that really financed much of Europe's development, a fact which is recognized by both historians and economists alike. The present financial system didn't exist at that time; the gold and silver came from Latin America. The resources contributed by the colonies—which also encompassed Africa and Asia—financed a large part of Europe's economic development. The former colonial powers have a moral obligation to the peoples whose wealth they siphoned off over the centuries.

It's not just the former colonial powers that are obligated; I believe all of the countries that have, in one way or another, achieved the privilege of development should express solidarity with the immense mass of humanity who have not been so fortunate, and who, by the mere accident of their births, are forced to dwell in areas of grinding poverty and dull hopelessness. I see this as the greatest moral imperative of our times. The great principles of fraternity among men so avidly proclaimed and inscribed in the great mottoes of the French Revolution—and the American Revolution—must now be resurrected for a modern audience. It is this very principle that lies at the heart of the New International Economic Order. It isn't just a matter of redress for historic injustices, for which we may or may not be responsible; rather, it is moral imperative that the human race take care of its own. If these ideas are taken as a starting point—the ideas of justice and solidarity among the people of the world—then international cooperation should be no problem in the New World Order.

Aside from this, injustice, inequality, inconsistency, and selfishness must cease between nations. If the industrialized capitalist countries really can't find solutions for their difficulties—because of their systems' intrinsic irrationality, anarchy, or internal contradictions—then I can find no justification for the protectionist policies that stunt the economies of the Third World countries, where billions of people live in almost subhuman conditions. If there is unemployment in the developed countries, it is due entirely to irrational policies, because if full employment existed—that is, if all human resources available were used—working men and women could share a shorter work week. (Rest is, after all, one of mankind's most prized possessions.) Dumping cheap goods is an even more reprehensible practice, because it constitutes unfair competition based on financial and technological superiority over countries with inherently weaker economies, nations desperately in need of the means of human subsistence.

Unequal terms of trade, the deadly process through which the commodities of the vast majority of the Third World countries bring ever lower prices, while the products they import from the industrialized countries become ever more expensive—a continually progressive historical trend—is one of the most diabolical expressions of the present system of economic relations imposed on the world. You can't call it anything but the systematic robbery of our peoples' resources and the fruits of their labors. Products produced almost exclusively by the Third World—coffee, cacao, precious wood, tea, spices, aluminum, copper, iron, manganese, chrome, medicinal plants, peanuts, sesame seeds, cashew nuts, coconuts, kenaf, sisal, or rubber—are frequently generated without mechanization, with very low productivity, grain by grain, leaf by leaf, in 12- or 14-hour workdays, with the labor of men, women, children, adolescents, and old people.

For example, sugar is, with very few exceptions, cut and loaded by hand and transported by oxcart. In general, all of the work is done in temperatures of 90 degrees or more, in humid climates, with seasonal work and starvation wages that don't amount to much more than $60 or $80 a month. The workers have no medical care, and large families live in thatched-roof huts with dirt floors, going barefooted most of the time and poorly dressed all the time, with no unemployment compensation and beggarly pensions, if they receive any pensions at all. Life expectancy is frequently less than 40 years, and there is a plethora of premature aging, lack of education, few recreational facilities—in other words, no comfort and no hope. Yet, in order to keep producing and just stay alive, the Third World still must import high-technology, industrially-processed products—even in the case of medical equipment and supplies—sales that help generate high company profits in the industrialized states. With the prices they charge us, we pay for the companies' profits, high executive salaries, taxes, unemployment compensation, old-age pensions, social benefits, and advertising.

We often have to pay 10, 15, or 20 times as much for our own raw materials that have been refined or processed than we receive for them. What do we get for our products?—very low wages, no social security or unemployment compensation, no medical care, no education, no culture, no recreation, no hope of progress, and premature aging and early death. And things are getting steadily worse: the same amount of coffee, sugar, tea, copper, iron, and bauxite that used to buy a particular piece of medical equipment, a medicine, an irrigation pump, a bulldozer, a crane, a truck, a tractor, or a simple work tool 35 years ago, now buys only a third as much. Every day there is more work; every day there are more sacrifices; every day there is more hunger for more people; every day there is more poverty. The New International Economic Order, as adopted by the United Nations, was designed to solve or at least mitigate these problems.

We have obtained fair and stable prices for our exports, which are now indexed to the prices of the products we import, in our relations with the socialist camp; and this has helped our industrial, agricultural, and especially our social development. With an average educational level of the ninth grade, an infancy death rate of only 15 children out of every 1000 born alive, a life expectancy of 73.5 years, and the fact that 85% of all Cuban homes now have electricity are just some of the results which compare favorably with those in the rest of Latin America. These achievements could not have been realized without much sacrifice and more equable terms of trade—not even with a fair social regime in power to force a more equal distribution of social wealth.

I've presented here just a few of my ideas about the New International Economic Order. Important concepts have also been advanced by others regarding the sharing of technological wealth, contributions of financial resources to assist the growth of Third world economies, and many others.

It's not so much a question of the industrial world—the U.S., for example, transferring its industrial or financial resources to the Third World—I'm realistic enough to understand that many countries couldn't do without them, no matter what the circumstances. Rather, it's a matter of immediately ending the huge transfers of resources which take place every year from Latin America (and the rest of the undeveloped states) to the industrialized world, amounting, as I have said, to more than $70 billion. No less than $50 billion of this is in hard cash, under various guises: interest on the debt, the flight of capital, interest spread, and the overvaluation of the dollar. When the Charter of the Economic Rights and Duties of States was discussed in the United Nations 10 years ago, this couldn't even be imagined to its fullest extent. As an immediate measure, the cancellation of the foreign debt is absolutely necessary. The United Nations proposed this a decade ago for a group of countries who were having the greatest difficulties. Now, there are very few Third World countries—if any—who don't have great difficulties. Today, they are divided into just two categories: those with great difficulties and those you would call "basket cases." Therefore, the cancellation of the debt and its interest must occur, if only to accommodate your much touted "Christian charity."

The industrialized world will lose nothing if the New International Economic Order is adopted by the world, just as it was approved a decade ago in the United Nations.

When a European Economic Community country wants to solve the economic problems of a small portion of its farming sector, it resorts to subsidies, not only to support its own domestic growers, but also to export considerable quantities of relatively cheap products, such as sugar, meat, or other foodstuffs, all markets in which the Third World countries must compete with their products.

It doesn't concern them that they are depressing the prices of basic exports from which hundreds of millions of people in the underdeveloped countries live, thereby depriving them of their livelihoods or even (in some cases) their lives. They don't have guilty consciences—it doesn't even occur to them what they are doing. They aren't the least bit bothered about raising the cost of those products for their own domestic customers, or about violating the principles of the free market system, not to mention free domestic and international trade, which are the bases of the philosophy for which they have fought many bloody wars. Eschewing these brutal neocolonialist practices would scarcely affect the industrialized countries; but it would promote a healthier, more stable, and more sustained development for the entire world economy.

For centuries, many believed that the end of colonialism would ruin Europe. On the contrary, history has shown that Europe has never before developed so much or achieved such high living standards as they have today, long after the collapse of the colonial system. In Asia, too, the catastrophic collapse of the empire of the Rising Sun—which sought to guarantee raw materials, rubber, oil, and other resources by force—marked the beginning of Japan's greatest economic development, prosperity, and well being. When, instead of exploiting others, nations have been forced to live off their own work and ingenuity, they have achieved unexpected wealth. Spain had one of greatest colonial empires. All of Spanish America contributed fabulous sums of gold, silver, and other wealth to Spain for 300 years. Did Spain develop? All that wealth wound up in England, France, Holland, and other countries. In the era of industrialization, Spain remained the most underdeveloped country in Europe until the beginning of this century. Did the colonies help in the development of Spain? They helped in the development of Europe, but Spain did not seem to benefit. The industrial development of Spain began toward the end of the last century, when it lost many of its colonies, including Cuba, the last colonial gold cup.

Another example is a recent development that began in 1974. During the sudden spectacular rise in oil prices, which went from $2.50 to $30 a barrel, many pundits felt that the economies of the industrialized countries could not withstand such price increases. Those most affected, however, were the non-oil-producing countries of the Third World, for whom a new form of unequal exchange emerged. Oil that cost the equivalent of 1 ton of sugar 20 years ago now cost 2½ times more. The same is true of coffee, cacao, sisal, fibers, fruits, minerals—everything the Third World countries produce. Tanzania, to name one case, is a country that lives off many of these products, and even exports meat produced from nomad herds. All of its exports together are not now sufficient to pay for its modest oil consumption, which is less than 1 million tons a year for a population of 18 million.

And what happened in the industrialized countries? Very little. They adapted—they developed programs to conserve the energy they were squandering; they designed more efficient engines; they started using coal once again; they developed nuclear energy; and they started to mine old coal pits or oil deposits which had ceased to be profitable. As a result of the energy hikes, they spent, in an 11-year-period, some $1 trillion to adapt to the new situation. Where did that money go? To U.S. and European banks—it returned to the industrialized capitalist countries. They handled it, lent it, increased exports to oil-exporting countries, made deals worth millions, and also sold unprecedented amounts of weapons. The Shah of Iran multiplied his purchases of weapons from the United States; the United States sold Saudi Arabia and Iran tens of billions of dollars worth of planes, radar equipment, and other arms. It was a sad situation, and they made a killing, if you'll pardon the expression. The price of oil most affected the already weak economies of the non-oil-producing Third World countries. So, what economic impact would cancellation of the debt have for the United States and the other industrialized countries? They would ultimately benefit, of course. Actually, I think it would result in a much fairer system that could significantly increase trade in agricultural equipment, medical equipment and machinery, and many other industrial and agricultural items. If the Third World receives fairer prices for its basic exports, the western industrialized countries would soon see increased sales and employment, and a marked growth in industrialized development throughout the world. All of this is possible. We only have to give up one thing: the madness of war and the arms race. Is this not obvious?

But if we want to be madmen, if we want to continue the arms race and maintain an unfair economic order, we will continue along the path leading to inevitably large-scale famine, great social conflict, and—more than likely—a large-scale nuclear holocaust, until all people, sane and insane, are wiped off the face of the Earth. Still, I hope, not all madmen are in government, and not all who govern are mad.

II.

THE POLITICAL CRISIS
IN CENTRAL AMERICA

ELLIOT: Let's turn to several other issues. Do you believe that the United States will invade Nicaragua?

CASTRO: Unfortunately, the possibility exists. It seems inconceivable to me that the United States would make such a stupid mistake. Irrespective of the fact that such an action would constitute a violation of every international law on the books—which has not stopped Reagan before—it's senseless to invade a country to solve a problem which can be handled perfectly well through existing peaceful channels, such as serious negotiation. I think solutions for the problem of Central America do exist, solutions which would satisfy the interests of Nicaragua, of the Central American countries, and of the United States itself.

Nicaragua is a member of the Latin American community. I think the example of the Malvinas/Falkland Islands War is somewhat appropriate, since Britain's military actions resulted in Spanish America rushing to Argentina's support, despite the fact that the Argentinian government was an indefensible, isolated, and thoroughly discredited government. There was a deep sense of solidarity.

These are new times; we are no longer living in the 1920s and '30s, when the United States could intervene at will in Santo Domingo, Haiti, Cuba, Central America, or Nicaragua without protest. In those days you would intervene, not out of fear of communism, but purely to safeguard American economic interests. Now, the mass media, combined with a greater awareness on the part of our people of their rights, would prevent a silent incursion. You must remember, at that time there were no United Nations or Organization of American States.

So, an intervention in Nicaragua would cause an enormous uproar in Latin America. The political situation in Central America can be described as a powder keg, similar to that of the Balkans prior to World War I. It would really be a great folly on the part of the United States to invade Nicaragua. You would have to commit genocide, killing tens of thousands of men, women, and children, in full view of the international media, including television and film. No matter how many measures you might take, you wouldn't be able to hide the magnitude of the killing or the use of warships, bombers, tanks, and troops to kill innocent Nicaraguans.

Of course, an American intervention would also cost U.S. lives and U.S. dollars; inevitably, you would find yourselves becoming bogged down in an interminable fight against an unseen foe. The Nicaraguans are militant, patriotic, brave; what they lack in war materiel would be made up with determination. It would be another Vietnam all over again. Remember when Sandino and a handful of men resisted a U.S. invasion for many years?

The technology doesn't exist to counteract a popular resistance movement. This has been shown in Vietnam, in the Sahara, and elsewhere. The Spanish gave the Spanish Sahara to Morocco, perhaps thinking that the king would thus never reclaim Ceuta and Melilla, Spanish enclaves on Morocco's Mediterranean coast. There are now 200,000 Moroccan soldiers there, and they are as impotent in their drive to seize that desert country as you were in Vietnam. They are armed by the United States, with technical advice, sophisticated weapons, and radar that can detect a man's every movement. Nevertheless, they remain unable to conquer the interior, and, in the long run, are doomed to defeat. Meanwhile, the Saharan freedom fighters have been recognized by the majority of OAU (Organization of African Unity) member states.

Similarly, the Salvadorans have been fighting for 6 years against an army advised by the United States, supplied by you with planes and helicopters, and with a great deal of sophisticated military equipment. They have demonstrated their capability to adapt to U.S. strategy and technology, and also to the abundant military and economic resources which the United States provides the Salvadoran government.

There are many other examples in the world. Consider the case of Cuba itself: if you review the history of Cuba, a mere handful of men waged war in the 1890s against the combined forces of 300,000 Spanish soldiers in the central and eastern parts of the island. We were the Vietnam of the last century.

There is no technology capable of smashing movements of popular resistance, where people are motivated by patriotic and revolutionary ideas. The political and human price you would have to pay is so high that a U.S. invasion of Nicaragua seems inconceivable to me. In the face of American military superiority, its numerous aircraft carriers, its complete air and sea dominion of the area, the Nicaraguans would scarcely receive any help. All that the United States would have to do is establish a rigorous air and sea blockade. Cuba simply does not have the means to break such a blockade. In other words, it's impossible for us to give them any kind of military support under such circumstances.

Our own armed forces are largely of a defensive nature. Our strength is based on the Cuban people, on millions of organized people, on every square meter of land, in the cities and the towns, in the countryside, in the mountains and on the plains. Such forces are effective only in fighting a particular kind of war, a popular struggle against an outside invasion. Our air and sea forces are limited in scope—we can't afford expensive hardware. We know how to employ what we have in conjunction with our troops to fight an invasion of our country, but we do not have the means to counter a U.S. blockade. If Nicaragua was blockaded, we do not have the military means to break it. However, we do have plans, ways to resist, that we could give to the Sandinistas. We have developed in great detail a program to fight a war of attrition. We have studied everything.

The Nicaraguans also do not have offensive armed forces, nor would it make any sense for them to use theirs against any neighboring country. Such an incursion on their part would hand the United States a perfect pretext to intervene in Nicaragua.

We revolutionaries have demonstrated that we can be calm and rational, because we ourselves have U.S. troops and an illegal U.S. naval base on our territory. They have been there since the end of the Spanish occupation, when a puppet government installed by the U.S. rented Guantánamo to your President for 100 years. No, actually they didn't stipulate a time limit. In this case the 100-year maximum is the limit recognized by international law.

DYMALLY: If the United States did invade Nicaragua, would your government respond militarily?

CASTRO: With what? The United States knows—in fact, anyone with military experience knows—that Cuba just doesn't have the military might even to break our own economic blockade. We can and do resist the blockade and U.S. aggression, but anything further is utterly absurd. The Nicaraguans are basically in the same situation: we are all small countries in an area where the United States has overwhelming superiority in conventional air and naval weapons, not to mention nuclear weapons. This does not crush, discourage, or intimidate us, but we are not stupid. An attack on Cuba might ultimately be a defeat for the United States but it would also be very costly for us. It's the kind of glory I just don't want. The U.S. would need millions of soldiers to occupy Cuba—I don't think you could do this unless you exterminated the entire country. You could drop a few nuclear bombs and wipe us off the face of the Earth—but that's not a defeat, it's a massacre. History would judge. A defeat is when you surrender and lower your flag. Exterminating us would be a Pyrrhic victory, at best, and I think America is smarter than that. Our philosophy is also the philosophy of the Nicaraguans and the Salvadorans. They won't surrender either, even if you spend $100 million in arms and economic help to the Salvadoran army.

ELLIOT: What in your opinion is the ultimate goal of American policies in Nicaragua?

CASTRO: The U.S. wants to destroy the Sandinista Revolution, just as it tried to destroy the Cuban Revolution, the independence of North Vietnam, and the Revolution in South Vietnam, just as the French sought to maintain their rule over Indochina and Algeria. France has one of the most advanced military forces in Europe. Algeria is a country which was 85% illiterate, and almost entirely filled with desert. Still, the Algerian people fought and won their independence. There have been many such wars; history tells us that the result, in most cases, was a victory for the underdog. Is this not true even in U.S. history?

    The notion that Nicaragua is somehow a threat to the United States, is nonsense. A small impoverished nation with a population of 3 million, a country which is among the poorest in Latin America, with a huge debt of hundreds of thousands of millions of dollars, a land destroyed both by the Somoza regime and earthquakes, could not seriously threaten the security of the United States in a thousand years.

DYMALLY: Then why not let the people of Nicaragua decide, with free elections and a competitive party system?

CASTRO: But that's just what the Nicaraguans did! In a framework of the strictest rules of liberal, bourgeois, western elections, whatever you want to call them, they had an election. They were asked to move up the date for the elections, which they did, with direct balloting and the participation of all parties that wished to participate. They even provided financial help to organized opposition groups.

    So what has happened as a result? When the United States realized that the right-wing parties would lose the election and the Sandinistas would be the clear winners, right from the start they began to discredit the whole process, demanding that the elections be delayed. The Sandinistas were faced with the problems of internal war and economic pressures—and the elections. Still, they submitted themselves to this trial by fire, and passed.

They also knew they would win the elections. They were convinced that they had the support of the people, just as the United States was convinced that its parties, its pupils in Nicaragua, would lose the elections. It was the U.S. government that encouraged Cruz to pull out and sabotage the elections. They also tried to have the liberals, and Godoy withdraw as well. By leaving the Sandinistas without opposition, the elections would be tainted in world opinion.

The United States didn't dare accept a true electoral challenge. Even though it complained constantly it refused to allow its parties to compete directly. They could have lost—and lost badly. It wasn't the Nicaraguans who rejected the democratic elections, even though they are a farce in many countries. In the U.S. itself, advertising agencies often have as much to do with the outcome of a campaign as the viability of parties or their candidates. Hundreds of millions of dollars are spent to peddle prospective office-servers like so many Coca-Cola bottles. This is also true in much of Latin America.

The Sandinistas accepted the challenge of elections. It was the United States which turned down the challenge, trying to sabotage and discredit them. But more than 1000 observers and journalists actually saw the people go to the polls, and do so enthusiastically. More turned out to vote in Nicaragua on a percentage basis than did in the last election in the United States. In the U.S. elections, the turnout was just over 50%, while in Nicaragua it was between 70% and 80%. What's more, Ortega received a higher percentage of the votes cast than Reagan, about 67% of the total. If you add in the votes of the other parties who claim to be more leftist than the Sandinistas, those who voted for the "revolutionary slate" amounted to more than 70% of the people. So what right does the U.S. have to challenge the elections in Nicaragua?

There is a solution, of course. I am absolutely convinced that a negotiated political solution is possible in Nicaragua, based on the views of all sides. That is what the Contadora group is trying to accomplish, to find a solution to the problem of Central America. Who has opposed the formula proposed by the Contadora? The United States.

The United States claimed to support the group until the moment of truth when the Contadora delegates adopted an act that lays down difficult conditions and limitations for Nicaragua. Nicaragua accepted it. It was a brave decision. They accepted the Contadora Act, but the United States has rejected it and has subsequently mobilized its allies in the area to contest the movement.

You ask what I think. I believe the United States still hopes to destroy the Nicaraguan Revolution from within in 3 ways. First, by excaerbating Nicaragua's own economic problems. Nicaragua's economic ills are the same as those facing most of the other Latin American countries: the international economic crisis, low export prices, and a mounting foreign debt. The U.S. refuses to help Nicaragua, and by its active inaction makes a bad situation worse.

Second, by imposing harsh economic sanctions against the Sandinistas. Nicaragua has been deprived of its sugar quota—as was Cuba—and is now left with a harvest it cannot easily sell. The United States was Nicaragua's major foreign market.

Third, by infiltrating and supporting counterrevolutionary bands, comprising thousands of men organized, trained, and supplied by the CIA, whose main strategy is to undermine the economy, sabotage the coffee harvest, industrial installations, and hamper transportation. This has, of course, had an effect. Coffee production has been lowered by 30%-35%, and the fish, timber, and legume industries have been decimated.

The United States government hopes the Nicaraguans won't be able to hold out, and that the combination of economic problems and armed counterrevolutionary bands will destroy the Sandinista Revolution from within. I don't think the United States is actually considering a direct invasion at the moment, but that's just my personal opinion. That danger will be highest when you realize that the Nicaraguan Revolution can't be destroyed from within, because, while production in Nicaragua may not be at 100%, it is still at 70% or 75% of normal, and they are now receiving help from abroad, including various western countries, among them Spain, and the socialist countries. The seven ships which the Pentagon claimed were taking weapons to Nicaragua did not contain a single bullet. They actually carried essential relief supplies, oil, food (such as wheat and rice), construction material, chemical products, and fertilizer, all of which the Nicaraguans need, and which—if well-administered—will enable them, together with what they produce themselves, to endure this economic crisis. The Contras, on the other hand, will never be able to defeat the Sandinista army.

DYMALLY: Apart from advisers, has Cuba provided direct military assistance to Nicaragua?

CASTRO: We have helped the Nicaraguans where we could, although, of course, not with military troops. There is not a single Cuban military unit in Nicaragua. They are quite capable of defending themselves, I think. All we have sent are advisers, instructors, teachers, and similar people, mostly volunteers, I should add.

ELLIOT: How many Cuban advisers are presently in Nicaragua?

CASTRO: I don't have the right to say how many there are. I will say that we have provided some military cooperation in the areas I have previously mentioned, because the Nicaraguans requested assistance in building a new army. They had no trained officers, no professional cadres, because the officers who had gone through their service academies all were loyal to Somoza. They had to start from scratch, training hundreds of thousands of citizens for local defense, so they asked for teachers, instructors, and advisers, and we have provided them as best we could.

DYMALLY: If you won't give us numbers, will you at least say whether you intend to increase the Cuban contingent there?

CASTRO: I think our group is probably sufficient for now, but I really shouldn't mention specific figures. Some time ago, I made the mistake of giving an interviewer approximate figures, and I don't intend to do it again. I don't object if the Nicaraguans want to, but it just doesn't seem right to me that we should be doling out such information without Nicaragua's advance approval. Would it not embarrass you to admit that you had to accept charity to survive? I've been in that situation myself, and I will not do something similar to a friendly state. Besides, what we're talking about here isn't just military cooperation. Our main form of assistance is civilian. Recently, we opened a modern sugar mill, one of the best factories of its kind in Central America, built in a very brief period of time. We supplied about 65% of the equipment directly from our plants in Cuba, plus equipment we had purchased from socialist countries, 80% and more of the components. We also provided the blueprints, technicians, engineers, and construction workers to help the relatively inexperienced Nicaraguans. When the facility was opened, we wanted to donate it to Nicaragua.

All of our previous assistance to Nicaragua had been in the form of donations of labor and materiel. But when the mill was constructed, they asked us to give them credit for its construction because they didn't want to keep taking our charity. So we did what they wanted—I, too, have my pride. At the time, their production was on the increase, including coffee, their chief export. Things looked good. Then came U.S. intervention and the outright hostility which interrupted their trade-lines, with production being affected directly. We took stock of the situation and said: "Well, they obviously have several economic problems; the best thing to do would be to cancel the debt." So we did. Cuba renounced the credit and cancelled the debt on the mill. We have since helped them with the construction of roads, bridges, and other projects.

ELLIOT: What other assistance have you provided?

CASTRO: We also have aided them in education and public health. We now have hundreds of doctors and health personnel working there. They are particularly needed, because the war has generated its wounded—they need surgeons; so our surgeons are there along with other types of doctors. Cuban doctors and health personnel also care for the large mass of Nicaraguans who have never had such services before.

We cooperate in the fields of agriculture and sports, and our assistance is basically civilian. I used the term, "economical aid," but I also meant to include education, health services, and related areas. We also train cadres, and have turned out about 1500 teachers. There is some military cooperation between the two states. This seems very fair to me. No one has a right to contend it, least of all the United States, which, in violation of international norms, is organizing, training, supplying, and directing mercenary bands against the people and the government of Nicaragua. Can our right to give them relatively modest defense aid be challenged? The Nicaraguans bear the brunt of this struggle, as shown by the fact that thousands have died as a result of the Contras' attacks—the majority of them civilians—including women and children. They attack a busload of civilians here, a truck there, villages, crops, and result is that many more civilians than soldiers have been killed, about 4000 people in all. This is only on the Sandinista side. We must also take into account the Nicaraguans who have been misled into joining the Contra groups; about 8000 or 9000 of them have died in this dirty war organized by the United States.

Although a solution to Nicaragua exists, the United States won't seriously negotiate or support the Contadora initiative so long as it hopes to destroy the Sandinista Revolution from within. This is a tragic fact, and is also why there have been no serious negotiations and will be none in the future. If the United States seriously wants a solution to this conflict, there will undoubtedly be a peaceful settlement in Central America which will satisfy all parties: Nicaragua, the Central American people, and the United States.

DYMALLY: Do the Sandinistas intend to create a Cuban-like political and economic system in Nicaragua?

CASTRO: Nothing could be further from the truth. I know the views of both the Sandinistas and the Salvadorans, though we have more contact with the former, because it is an established government.

Nicaragua has a much lower level of development than Cuba did at the time of the Revolution. Cuba had a larger working class, hundreds of thousands of agricultural workers, hundreds of thousands of industrial workers, a much more developed working environment. Nicaragua is more backward. It has many craft industries, and many people who still earn a living from petty trading. The conditions are different, the culture different, even the language is spoken with a different accent. You Americans often make the erroneous assumption that all the Latin American countries are alike.

The Nicaraguans know that their struggle is basically a struggle for independence, national liberation, and social progress; that they need to implement agrarian reform, educate the entire population, and provide everyone with health care. Economic development is the top priority for the Nicaraguan government, not the construction of socialism.

DYMALLY: Still, isn't it true that the Sandinistas are establishing a socialist system, of whatever stripe?

CASTRO: Actually, that's not a short or even a medium-term objective of their government, and it's certainly not on their current agenda. I think the Nicaraguan plan—and I have no disagreements with it—is perfect, given the conditions in their country and in Central America. Perfect!

This doesn't mean that the Nicaraguans aren't revolutionary— they *are* revolutionary. It would be a mistake to think that they are mere reformists, mere patriots or democrats who don't want to transform their country in a social sense.

They would not renounce, just as no revolutionary would renounce, the ultimate objective of transforming their society and establishing a socialistic system when socialism is finally possible. Their Revolution will eventually go as far as any other social revolution. For now, however, they have no plans of establishing a socialistic regime in Nicaragua. Their organization is called the Sandinista National Liberation Front, not the Socialist Party. That is why I told you that their current priorities are a series of reforms in societal structure. I think that agrarian reform is the most important element of this. Of course, they nationalized the holdings of the Somoza family; they did not nationalize the bourgeoisie's property, because in Nicaragua there wasn't any bourgeoisie. Somoza was the one who owned most of the industry in Nicaragua, and they confiscated his holdings because they had been obtained through theft; of course, they were not then given to the transnationals or to private enterprise. I don't think the Sandinistas can be criticized because they confiscated Somoza's property—many of you in America would have done the same—or because they didn't promptly hand it over to American private firms. There is still an oil refinery owned by an American company; foreign firms have been allowed to keep their property, and there are no plans to nationalize them. If it were I, perhaps I would have acted differently—my point is, however, that the Sandinistas made their own decisions, and submit to paternalism no more willingly than you would. There have been a series of structural changes in government, a program of economic and social development. This is not a fairy tale designed to fool anybody. Their methodology corresponds to the reality of Nicaragua, and I agree with it completely. Of course, if Cuba gives them financial and technical help for the construction of a sugar mill, they won't end up handing it over to a private company. But, in many countries, among them México, oil is state-owned, the petrochemical industry is state-owned, the iron and steel industry is state-owned. In Nicaragua, the state controls foreign trade and general financial resources. This has also been done by various capitalist countries, although I understand that there are private banks in Nicaragua. But financial control is not held by the private banks—it is held by the state. Control of foreign trade is not held by private institutions—foreign trade is in the hands of the state.

They must develop the country—that is their only program. This includes agricultural, industrial, and energy development. They see this as their fundamental task, one in which private enterprise will also have its role to play. They even plan to draft a law on foreign investment. There are sectors where they do not have the technology or financial resources to expand their economy themselves, so I suppose it will be necessary to use foreign resources and companies in those cases; even in Cuba, there are situations in which foreign technology and investments are necessary.

Development is the main objective of Nicaragua, since it is very difficult to have socialism without development. Of course, it must be the kind of development that does not benefit capitalism, and is not carried out with the supervision of capitalistic landlords and economists. It will be development under the leadership of a revolutionary government which serves the people, and not foreign oligarchs or overseas companies, which is what we see elsewhere in our hemisphere. This is the program of a mixed economy and political pluralism, a political pluralism without fear.

Nicaragua is now drafting a constitution. I can't say what kind of a constitution it will be, but I think it will reflect the realities mentioned here. I would not even think of interfering in this process.

ELLIOT: Do the Salvadoran rebels share the same objectives as the Sandinistas?

CASTRO: I think they're very similar. Of course, El Salvador has a little more industrial development than Nicaragua, but I haven't heard the Salvadorans talk of socialism. What they do want is to rid themselves of a genocidal system in which a small group of 30 or 40 families effectively own most of the country. Otherwise, I suspect the Salvadorans have more or less the same plans as the Nicaraguans; in fact, I think most of the other nations in Latin America, once liberated, will hesitate before embracing a fully-socialistic system. They have other, much more pressing problems, including finding enough food to keep their people alive.

The two basic issues facing Latin America are true independence and economic development. Latin America won't really be independent unless it can break the economic apron strings tying it to the industrialized world. True development must include social and cultural development, as well as economic. Those Latin American countries where multinational corporations have made huge investments have attained certain levels of production, but most have little or no social development. Illiteracy still exceeeds 30% in much of Spanish America, and combined with semi-literacy, may include a figure as high as 80% of the total population. Sanitary conditions are terrible. Infant mortality is high. Life expectancy low. The problems are endless. Of course, neither the governmental oligarchs nor the highranking military officers, both of whom serve only themselves and the foreign interests, want true independence. The people are the ones who must fight for it.

Although I'm not a prophet, I think the other Latin American countries will, to a greater or lesser degree, follow the Nicaraguan model. Their program is neither a pretext nor a lie. I think the challenge they have set for themselves is admirable. Why? Because they trust in the people, they will always have the support of the people.

The secret of remaining in power is not to be found in constitutional mechanisms or electoral systems. In the Cuban system, which is very different from that in Nicaragua, the Revolution would quickly vanish if we lost the support of the people. In our elections, the people themselves put forward their candidates at the grassroots level, and those delegates are the ones who in turn elect municipal, provincial, and national bodies. Keeping office is not dependent on electoral whim or television advertising; it's a matter of holding the support of the people. If you have that, you can retain power. no matter what mechanism you use. That's a fact not even the most rabid defender of your system can deny.

So, the Nicaraguans accepted the challenge to conduct traditional, open elections, like those held in the United States and other Latin American countries. I don't have to tell you that free elections are rare in the histories of Guatemala, El Salvador, and Nicaragua; from the time of Walker, the U.S. pirate who made himself dictator there in the mid-nineteenth century, one finds a series of military regimes, dictatorships, American and British interventions, and remarkably few democratically-elected governments. The only exception to this pattern is Costa Rica. For 100 years the United States never worried about democracy in Central America—it only became a factor when revolution broke out in Central America. It's amazing how "concerned" you suddenly become when it suits your interests.

DYMALLY: I don't see any of the other Latin American countries rushing to embrace the Nicaraguan model.

CASTRO: I am refering to future social changes in Latin America that will inevitably come to pass. I am not speaking of any country in particular, since, as I have already said, I am not a prophet. I speak, rather, of those countries in general, where the people have found and will find the courage to wrest power from the oligarchs, the representatives of big capital, or traditional army officers. I should mention, however, that the army has played a progressive role in both Perú and Panamá. So we can't generalize too much when we talk about the Latin American armed services, since we don't know what role they might play in bringing about these changes. In some places they will be very reactionary, in others very progressive.

ELLIOT: Is Cuba supplying arms to the Salvadoran rebels?

CASTRO: I replied to that question earlier. I will neither affirm nor deny our aid. For the time being, they have and will continue to receive our political solidarity and our support, in all arenas, including the international one. As far as military aid is considered, it's almost physically impossible for arms to reach the Salvadorans. So a discussion of this topic is almost metaphysical.

DYMALLY: Almost impossible is not quite the same as impossible.

CASTRO: I didn't say that it was completely impossible, just almost impossible. I can say that it is practically impossible and that the issue is almost metaphysical—I say "almost" because we're discussing a theoretical problem. Helping the Salvadorans for me is a moral issue, since the Salvadorans are fighting a regime that practiced systematic genocide, having murdered some 50,000 of their fellow countrymen in the last ten years. The Salvadorans are fighting for their political lives. I personally believe that their cause is just, and that the right of another country—or its leader—to help a neighbor, a movement, and a people who are fighting against genocide is paramount.

By what moral principle can the United States deny our right to support El Salvador, when it organizes, supplies, and arms thousands of Contras in Nicaragua? Don't tell me we can't send aid to El Salvador. In practical terms the question is moot, since it's almost impossible to reach the areas where the Salvadoran rebels have their camps. Perhaps this is to their ultimate advantage. When we struggled here in Cuba against Batista's army of 70,000 men, we did so without foreign aid, with the weapons and ammunition we captured from Batista's troops. It was more than ample.

The main supplier of the Salvadoran revolutionaries is, ironically enough, the U.S. Pentagon, because a large part of the weapons and ammunition America sends to El Salvador ends up in the hands of the rebels. Thus, when I speak of the Salvadorans' capacity to resist the U.S.-supported government indefinitely, I am talking about their capacity to fight under the worst possible conditions, in which they receive not a single rifle or bullet from abroad.

They seem to have adapted perfectly well to the difficult circumstances, responding to all the tactics and strategies of the U.S.-advised Salvadoran army. They can survive indefinitely without any foreign aid. More important than the question of whether or not they receive aid from abroad is the one of whether or not they can survive without it. I believe they can.

ELLIOT: Do you see a military solution to the Nicaraguan war?

CASTRO: Never! There is no possible military conclusion that would satisfy U.S. interests. On the other hand, there are many potential political solutions that would benefit Nicaragua, the people of Central America, and, of course, ultimately, the United States.

DYMALLY: Will the current trend towards democratic government in Latin America help Cuba's relationships with these nations?

CASTRO: It's not really a major factor so far as I can see. We have never subordinated the question of Cuba's diplomatic ties to our basic interests, or even the interests of the countries themselves. I think that each of these countries should do what it considers most appropriate. If it's in their interests to reestablish ties with Cuba, I'm sure they'll do so; if not, I won't lose any sleep over it. We have never tried to pressure any country (including the U.S.) in this regard, and we never will. More important than any diplomatic relations is the consolidation of the democratic process itself. I feel everyone should help these states in every way possible—we will certainly do our share.

Reagan may say that democracy is advancing everywhere, but what is really moving forward is the U.S. system of domination in Latin America. The process signifies that military dictatorships are on a permanent decline; that resorting to repression and force to maintain the old system has failed; and that the murders, the sophisticated torture, the kidnappings—things the United States taught the armies and the police in Latin America—that all these atrocities no longer will maintain that system. The crisis has become so profound that the armed services now understand that these countries have become unmanageable.

ELLIOT: What about Guatemala?

CASTRO: I can't say it's a typical case. Guatemala has serious economic, political, and social problems—yet it's very different from, say, the democracies of South America. The Southern Cone countries have greater industrial development and a higher social and political consciousness. Central America is poorer, more accustomed to a system of hereditary oligarchical families, military *caudillos*, and interminable military dictatorships.

In other words, the military tyrants in South America, realizing that the situation in those countries was becoming unmanageable, abdicated and transferred the reins of government to civilians after having totally failed in their leadership (and also, I should add, after having totally ruined the countries to a greater or lesser degree). They did not act from a sense of altruism, but only because they had been wholly discredited. But I do detect certain differences between the policy followed by the Brazilian services and those of the Chileans, Argentines, and Uruguayans, who opened their doors wide to competition and wiped out their own national industries. In any event, the crisis has become so profound that the armies no longer consider themselves capable of ruling.

DYMALLY: Isn't it true that the present situation is equally unmanageable for a civilian government?

CASTRO: They've certainly inherited a difficult situation in Argentina, with foreign debts of $45 billion; in Uruguay, the debt is $55 billion; in Brazil, $104 billion; and in Chile, where there will inevitably be changes, $22 billion. During the period of the Popular Unity government there, the Chilean debt was only $4 billion, the price of copper was higher, and still the situation was becoming very difficult. Of course, Allende's situation was compounded by his lack of foreign credit, which the United States had cut off. But now the civilian governments of South America are left with a tragic legacy. In Argentina, Uruguay, and Brazil, there will be further huge, unmanageable inflation or such stringent economic measures that society will eventually explode.

Perhaps the greatest accomplishment these military governments will be remembered for is that they turned all of their citizens into "millionaires." Inflation makes currency worthless. Living standards have declined considerably in all of these countries. It remains to be seen what effect the newly imposed controls will have in Brazil and Argentina.

ELLIOT: Would you like to see a major upheaval in Latin America?

CASTRO: Nobody knows what will happen if events keep moving in their current direction. The threat is not that the military will return to power; the danger is that Latin American societies will explode.

I will give you an example: in Bolivia, which has a president I really esteem, with every desire to salvage the democratic process, there is a Communist Party which is not involved in subversion, but which serves as an ally of the legitimate government, even participating in the coalition that won the last election there. And yet no government party seems able to control that segment of the labor movement which refuses to make new sacrifices. Inflation continues to increase, strikes are called one after the other, the social situation is untenable, and the Communists are not the ones creating the protest; it is the unions, workers, peasants, the people in general who can no longer stand the economic strain. You see there the presence of factors beyond the government's control. Who do you blame for subverting society? The people are no longer willing to accept the limitations on their standard of living. All this has happened because Bolivia's foreign debt must be paid, and the interest rates and the demands of the IMF must be met.

Four years ago, a civilian government came to power in Perú in elections in which they won more than half the votes cast, with a solid majority in Parliament. Now that same party has the support of only 3.8% of the voters. Alan García's Socialists will sweep the next election with a majority, but will how he handle Perú's debt and its many social problems? In Perú, there is a social upheaval which nobody seems to understand, but which is surely a reflection of its inherent internal crises and instability. Those are just two examples. In my opinion there will ultimately be social revolutions, for better or for worse, unless these issues are addressed.

DYMALLY: Would you prefer to see change arising from democratic processes or from a cataclysmic explosion?

CASTRO: I will try to present things as objectively as possible, as I see them.

When this issue came up recently, I said: "It is impossible to export the conditions which give rise to revolution." At the same time, we must recognize that the measures of the International Monetary Fund, Latin America's staggering foreign debts, the $40 bil-

95

lion in interest that accrues on that debt annually, the international economic crisis, the drop in prices realized by Latin American commodities, protectionism, and high interest rates, are all very subversive factors."

Even the Pope's trips are subversive, in a sense. When John Paul II visited India, he spoke to the poor people there of the need to provide land for the peasants, to build schools for their children, provide doctors and medicine for their sick, employment for those able to work, and three meals a day, adequate for the family's nutritional needs. All those things are subversive to the conditions of the underdeveloped nations of the hemisphere. If the Pope had visited Cuba, he would have had to talk about something else. Here 99% of our children go to school, and we already provide hospitals, doctors, and medications in ample supply. Everyone works who wants to, and nobody starves or suffers from malnutrition. His comments do reflect conditions in Venezuela despite its oil revenues, in Ecuador, Perú, and in all the cities and countrysides of the nations he visited. But how can this problem be solved? The Pope has said we must provide for the needs of our fellow man, and I agree with his sentiments. But we are faced throughout much of Latin America with unmanageable debts, underdevelopment, accumulated social problems, high interest rates, huge inequalities in the distribution of wealth, and a long series of other factors which have (perhaps unwittingly) been laying the groundwork for massive social unrest—or even revolution. If that happens, it will not be my fault.

DYMALLY: Still, you have been accused on many occasions of exporting the Cuban revolution to Latin America. Haven't you ever been tempted, in light of present realities, to light the torch that would ignite the social unrest that you claim exists?

CASTRO: There is no need. Revolution will start through spontaneous combustion, and then not all the water in the world will be enough to put it out.

I am not interested in preserving the existing social order: I think it must change. Nor am I interested in preserving a system of American rule over our people. The old ways do not work and cannot be preserved.

The explosiveness of this situation would be eased somewhat if the debt were to be cancelled, by agreement between the parties or by the unilateral action of the debtors. However, there is already an untenable situation in Latin America—this is reflected in the fact that the conservative factions are dying out in the hemisphere. If you talk to the conservatives, they hardly seem like conservatives any longer, and they show signs of frustration and desperation. The workers are desperate, and so are the middle classes. These sectors are very important in such crises.

I think the old order can no longer hold the system together. Something similar happened at the time of Latin American independence: all of the underlying factors were in place when Napoléon occupied Spain; this gave rise to patriotic juntas that were initially established as signs of loyalty to Spain, but ended in establishing the independence of this hemisphere.

I don't advocate one method or another—I think about events, and see what will happen. Perhaps it would be better—less wrenching and less bloody—for these changes to take place in a more orderly manner. I don't go around setting off social explosions, but I do think of what happened in other countries and eras. The situation in France in 1789 was very similar. French society exploded and there was a large and bloody convulsion.

ELLIOT: Isn't it true that some upheavals are reactionary rather than revolutionary?

CASTRO: I don't think so. That time has largely passed, although I can't say it won't happen in isolated cases. In the 1960s and '70s in Latin America, a number of right-wing military regimes took power, maintaining themselves through fascism, murder, torture, and kidnappings—and they ruined the nations they ruled. What is the alternative? In Brazil, the people mobilized many millions of their countrymen on the issue of direct voting; this was followed by the intelligent action of the political parties, who united these forces to win a victory in the electoral college which had been set up to nominate official governmental candidates. Suddenly we had a revolution, so to speak, in Brazil. It was not violent, but it was profound.

In my opinion, there is no new risk of a military *coup* in Argentina, Uruguay, or Brazil. There will always be some old-line military officers with political ambitions, maybe 8% or 10%, madmen who talk of *coups*; but the majority realize it would be crazy. But when there is social turmoil and the economy is uncertain, 90% may suddenly be inclined to mount a quick *coup*. That is not the case now: these countries are mired in crisis and the military realizes it can't run them. The possible resort to force does exist in isolated countries, such as the Dominican Republic, but elsewhere they seem to have run their course.

DYMALLY: What about Chile?

CASTRO: Chile is a volcano waiting to erupt. There the social convulsions were halted with brute force, but Pinochet doesn't have much time left either. The situation is most critical. Everybody opposes him; the people aren't afraid anymore. Even the United States doesn't trust Pinochet, because it fears another Nicaragua in South America. This is the country which I feel is closest to a much more profound social revolution if rebellion breaks out. The United States understands this and has been trying to ease him out, but has not been successful. Pinochet is very stubborn. We may yet see a popular revolution in Chile, if Pinochet's tenure drags on. You people always react after the fact. Kennedy showed concern after the triumph of the Cuban Revolution. Prior to the Revolution, however, nobody was interested in land reform, tax reform, or a social program for Latin America, because anybody who mentioned such things was accused of being a Communist. When Cuba rebelled, however, suddenly you began to worry. The people of this hemisphere owe a great deal to the Cuban Revolution. The U.S. said: "Well, let's introduce some reforms; let's do something before more revolutions erupt in this hemisphere," and it developed the Alliance for Progress, some 25 years ago.

How much time has passed, and how many new problems do we have now? Will they have the wisdom to be flexible? Anything's possible, although I wonder what the industrialized countries could do. They could absorb the debt with their own banks and give us some breathing space.

Perhaps some rational analysis and a more realistic approach to the situation might lead to an orderly, non-violent solution to the problem.

I even told your people—when they spoke of it—that a return to normal relations with Cuba would benefit Americans more than us. We can sit here quietly in the front row, so to speak, waiting to see what's going to occur and watching events as they unfold. It is to the advantage of the United States to change because you could at least show your capacity to adapt to current realities. When a profound social crisis breaks out—in Chile, Perú, Brazil, or Argentina—the United States would be powerless to prevent it. Such problems cannot be solved by landing a battalion of paratroopers under some fairy tale pretext, as you did in Grenada. Failing to understand such things can be very costly.

Why then has Central America exploded? Simply, because you were unable to foresee what was coming. You could have worked for political change years ago. You could have addressed the issues of underdevelopment, poverty, and oppression, and thereby you could have forestalled many of your present concerns. Now you want to intervene. What's going to happen in South America can also be foreseen, and again you say: "Let's do something about it." I say: this is the real world. We must all draw our own conclusions. Nothing would make me happier than to see the big international powers act sanely, prudently, absolutely, and wisely. And I certainly don't think I'm doing any harm by airing my views on these problems.

DYMALLY: If this is true, wouldn't it be contrary to Cuba's interests if the United States accepted your assessment and attempted to stifle the revolutionary process in Latin America?

CASTRO: I think it's tied up with the international situation, because the problem is not strictly Latin American. The economic crisis affects the entire world, including the industrialized countries, and, to a much larger measure, the Third World countries.

The non-aligned nations have said that Third World problems are desperately in need of a solution. In the past, just as many people died of starvation in Africa as now, but nobody heard about it. Now, suddenly, it's on American television. Of course, there have been revolutionary changes in several African countries, including Ethiopia, and Ghana, but one cannot speak of an explosive situation on a global scale. Africa's level of economic, social, and cultural development is lower than that of Latin America. The working class, the peasantry, and the cultural elite are less developed there than here. Africa does not have a large and extended middle class, and it also lacks doctors, economists, teachers, lawyers, engineers, or architects, and universities to train those professionals. Africa's people are paying in the harshest coin the consequences of underdevelopment, economic crisis, and natural disasters. Whatever changes may have occurred there have neither the magnitude nor the repercussions of those in Latin America.

We must also take into account the danger of war and the arms race. If the problems we're talking about are to be solved, such ideas as military superiority, "Star Wars," outrageous military expenditures, and a frenzied arms build-up must go—they are incompatible with any real solution to the world's economic and social problems. The idea is to seek peace, international détente, coexistence, and even cooperation among countries. In other words, averting war is a necessity in bringing about social change.

All these problems are closely interrelated, and they demand a basic change in the ways people think, particularly in the industrialized capitalist countries. The United States must play a leading role in taking the initiative. Twenty years ago, you talked about the "yellow peril," the threat of Communist China. Now, you are investing there, you have cordial relations with China, and the "threat" has suddenly vanished. Just imagine what would happen if socialist China suddenly reverted to old China, with its hundreds of millions of hungry people.

Socialist China feeds and clothes its own people, and the United States is now delighted with its relations with her. You've changed your attitude towards China. Why is it so difficult for you to change your attitudes in Latin America? What I have said about Latin America forms part of a broader analysis of the world's problems, of war and peace, the arms race and economic development. I think that the only way to tackle the problem of underdevelopment is through the cooperation of the entire international community: the socialist and the capitalist countries working together. Peace alone will not solve the problem of underdevelopment. Its solution is to be found in a kind of peace that does not consist solely of reducing the number of nuclear arms, or abrogating a "Star Wars" program, but in a genuine willingness to raise millions of human beings out of poverty by using the resources which are so readily available to us. All men are equally worthy to share in the world's bounty. I can't help but wonder if the persistence of certain attitudes on the part of your government is not, at its heart, just another form of racism. The Monroe Doctrine is another way of saying you Norte Americanos are inherently superior to those of us who spead different languages and have differently colored skins (*i.e.*, darker). The fact is, you have no more right to involve yourselves in Cuba's (or in any other country's) affairs then we do in yours. The principle of noninterference in other countries' internal politics is sacrosanct. There should be no involvement on the part of either the United States or Cuba. Let every country in this region assume responsibilty for whatever political and economic system it decides to follow, and let no one try to inject a new social system from outside or to prop up an unjust social order that's about to collapse. In other words, gentlemen, allow us the same right you trumpet so loudly to the rest of the world—the right of each nation to choose its own destiny.

ELLIOT: In your view, then, is revolution inevitable?

CASTRO: In Chile, the United States and the CIA spent millions of dollars to put Pinochet in power. What have you solved by doing this? Was not the United States the instigator of the ugly *coup d'état* in Brazil that overthrew the democratically-elected government of President Joao Goulart? America trained and advised Latin America's greatest thugs and torturers.

Now, the United States is trying to crush a revolutionary movement in El Salvador, while in Nicaragua it is using mercenaries to overturn a legitimately-elected regime. Did your earlier interventions in Brazil, Chile, Argentina, and Uruguay solve anything? Why don't you give the Latin American people a chance to develop their own voices without interference? The United States must learn from its past mistakes. But if it doesn't have that capacity, I can tell you exactly what's going to happen.

If you talk with the people who live in Latin American, you'll find there are few conservatives left. You won't even notice a great difference between what a conservative tells you and what I say, when it comes to discussing the free enterprise system, the lifting of foreign trade barriers, or the competition between indigenous industry and overseas plants in the production of goods for internal consumption. They're horrified at the economic ruination of their countries. They don't want to even talk about western economic theories.

Free currency exchange has also been very costly to Latin America. I know of cases where people have borrowed large sums in their national currencies, exchanged the amount for American dollars, deposited the dollars in U.S. banks, earned higher interest there, and within a few months were able to pay back the original debt with only half of the American dollars. Faced with such realities, many people lose faith in classic, traditional mechanisms.

I've noticed something new in those Latin Americans who have visited Cuba recently. There's a strong inner force that wasn't noticeable before. Last year, I met with hundreds of Latin American film directors, producers, actors, and actresses. They have to compete with U.S. productions. They produce excellent films, but can't even cover their production costs, because the U.S. transnationals control everything. You can't imagine how irritated these talented men and women were. The future belongs to the people of this continent. Europe is spent, politically and intellectually. The consumer society has its price. If our continent has enormously varying cultures and values, we also have many things in common, to the extent that there's a strong feeling of brotherhood among Latin American and Caribbean film producers, writers, and intellectuals, which doesn't exist in Europe or elsewhere.

DYMALLY: You recently have made an effort to make yourself more available to questioning by the western press. Do you foresee a relaxation in tensions between the United States and Cuba?

CASTRO: It's certainly possible. Something happened recently that should serve as a positive and constructive example of what can be done. I speak, of course, of the agreement on migration. It showed that difficult, complex problems can be solved when they are discussed seriously, with flexiblilty and respect for both sides of the question, as they were in this case. There were several incidents that delayed the process—not on our side, but from the United States. On several occasions, Reagan expressed a desire to return to Cuba a certain number of those people who had arrived in the

United States on the Mariel boatlift. We said that we were willing to discuss the matter within the general framework of migratory relations between the two countries.

When, in April of 1984, you agreed to discuss the problem under these conditions, we thought your response was merely part of your national election campaign, and didn't think about it too seriously. We were also concerned that the question would become a matter of public debate in the U.S. We therefore suggested that discussions be postponed until after the elections. Jesse Jackson brought the matter up again when he visited Cuba in June. We said we were willing to discuss it if the two American political parties were in accord, because we didn't want the matter to become an election year issue. Both the Democrats and the Republicans agreed, and so discussions began. The process was interrupted when an American spy plane flew over Cuba. Later, the talks were resumed. It's noteworthy that your government was willing to continue the talks even after the elections were over. Both sides adopted flexible positions, and an issue that had initially seemed very touchy was settled through mutual dialogue. Perhaps you thought that we wouldn't take back the criminals who had left our country, because you're aware of how our people feel about them.

However, the questions were ultimately settled to everyone's satisfaction. There's something else which I also view as positive in a general sense: Reagan made a speech couched in surprisingly peaceful terms following his inauguration. Also, I noted the United States' interest in finding some political formula to the problems of South Africa and Angola. Perhaps this reflects a more realistic approach on the part of the United States.

I certainly don't believe U.S. foreign policy is clearly defined. Rather, it seems to me that there are many contradictions. For example, Reagan's expressed willingness to negotiate with the Russians, while simultaneously insisting on the "Star Wars" program, the MX missile, and the B-1 bomber. Administration spokesmen appearing before the U.S. Congress justify their budget requests on the grounds that these programs will strengthen your bargaining position.

We are not certain whether these programs are merely tactical feints, or are designed as real offensive or defensive weapons. If they're the latter, there will be no *détente*, only a continuing colossal arms race which will have catastrophic effects on the world's economy, while simultaneously posing a serious danger to world peace. We also take note of what's happening in Nicaragua. There's too much insistence on the American side of an aggressive posture and on support for the Contras. I still believe that a desire for a political solution does exist in the U.S., but I also think there are many elements in your government which hope to liquidate the

Sandinista revolution. One can never completely be sure what you people really think. So, while I see some positive signs, the way has not yet been opened for a negotiated settlement of the crisis in Central America.

We believe it is possible to improve relations between the United States and Cuba in the framework of a more realistic peace policy on the part of the United States. However, we cannot leave ourselves cut off in an ivory tower. As long as the United States maintains an interventionist policy in Central America and is bent on invading Nicaragua, as long as the United States maintains a bellicose attitude toward the world in general, it would be almost utopian to speak of the possibility of improving relations between Cuba and the United States. We conceive of such an improvement as part of an improvement in international relations as a whole, and we have expressed our willingness to contribute to a political solution wherever possible, be it in South Africa, the Caribbean, or Latin America. We cannot obviously be a major factor in determining the outcome of certain problems, but we can contribute to the effort to find a solution. This is what we said to the foreign ministers of the Contadora Group.

We don't simply say that we support the Contadora—we say we support them for specific reasons. We view the Group's efforts as beneficial to Central America, to Nicaragua, and to the Caribbean area as a whole. At the same time, we realize that all these events have a bearing on the international situation.

I believe that anything that exacerbates the situation in one place has a similar effect elsewhere. Anything that improves one area will help improve the situation in another. Assuming that the United States has decided to take a more realistic approach, the Reagan government now has the authority to act; it won both elections by wide margins and presumably can now tackle even complex situations. It has often been the case in the United States that the government has lacked the necessary authority in its first term in office to do much more than vacillate on foreign policy. This frequently changes in a second term. The problems are so serious, not only in the United States but throughout the rest of the world, that a president lacking in authority would find it very difficult to put into practice the kind of policies we're talking about. There's certainly no danger of Reagan being accused by his enemies of Communist sympathies. He has the personal authority and voice to make whatever moves he wishes to reduce international tensions.

Such a policy would directly benefit the U.S. economy and that of the rest of the world. There's a growing concern in America over the economy, including the budget and trade deficits. If your government is going to solve these problems, you cannot really afford to engage in adventures abroad.

Some Americans say, "Let's see some hard evidence that Cuba means what it says." We don't have to prove anything, in my estimation. We don't need the U.S. to survive. We're in no hurry to improve relations. We're simply standing by our principles when we say serious negotiations will help bring about peace in Central America. You are the ones who must prove your sincerity with deeds, not words. You are the ones who are always saying, "We support Contadora, we support Contadora." A hundred times you've stated your support for the Group, and yet, when push came to shove, you sabotaged the Contadora Act. Cuba is a small country whose actions have no real effect on world politics. The United States, on the other hand, is a superpower; your actions are a determining factor in Latin America and in many other parts of the world.

Our words are also our deeds, because they correspond to our actions, and our actions our words. Moreover, we do not lie—we've never used such methods. Unfortunately, your government often resorts to deliberate obsfucation, prevarication, or confusion in your foreign policy statements. You're often wrong, but you never admit you're wrong. I recently saw a white paper issued by your executive branch to justify its request to Congress for money to wage a dirty war in Nicaragua, a request based on a pack of absurdities. It was followed by a document on the human rights situation in Nicaragua, in which your government had no qualms about making all sorts of inaccurate statements about Cuba and its role in Central America. When you can't use hard facts you resort to lying.

ELLIOT: Do you fear that improved relations with the United States would diminish the impact of the Cuban Revolution?

CASTRO: I'm not too worried about that. Our people have developed an awareness which is not based on chauvinism, nationalist extremism, or hatred for other people or even for the United States. No. Our Revolution is the cement which unites the people, which gives force to our ideas, which provides the moral and political values which motivate our people. We are not a nation of fanatics in any sense of the word. Fascism used fanaticism, nationalism, racial superiority, and even xenophobia to control the people. But we certainly have no need of such things. Yes, we have struggled and defended ourselves, and I think we've done so very well. I'm proud of what we've accomplished here. You won't find any personality cults or transformation of leaders into gods here. You won't find a street named after me, or a school, or a statue, or even my image on a public building; when somebody puts up a photo of me, it's because he or she wants to. We have never printed pictures of me for public offices. We are not inclined to dictatorship or personal rule. Your government calls me a *caudillo*, ignoring the fact that no one-man decisions are made here, that there are solid political and state institutions based on collective leadership of representatives nominated by the people. As I have said on other occasions, my only right as a government official is to speak my mind and outline my political views. I dictate nothing.

DYMALLY: Have you given any thought to resigning or stepping down from power?

CASTRO: No, I don't plan to resign, because for me it's just a job, like being a doctor, architect, engineer, or even a common laborer. I will do it as long as I feel useful. I am really more experienced now than when I started, and it probably wouldn't benefit Cuba to replace me with someone less experienced now; I've had my apprenticeship just like anyone else.

But I'm not worried about the future, nor do I feel it's essential for me to have this position. I am absolutely convinced that there are many new people—an entire new generation—coming to the fore, and they should be given their own opportunities. In order for somebody to do this particular job, all that's needed is that he or she be assigned the task. I saw that during the Revolution many comrades, even those who were in the troops, would rise to the occasion. Sometimes you had to work with them on the question of discipline; when they knew someone else was worrying about it they didn't give the matter much thought. But when they themselves were given the task of leading a column, they suddenly became excellent and well-disciplined commanders. You have to give such a person the opportunity to develop his abilities. My philosophy is this: I know there are many capable people here; I know that the value of any particular individual is relative; and I am relaxed about the future because I know that someone else can do my job.

We have a collective leadership here. There are no one-man decisions. There's even an established system by which appointments are made. It's not as if I say, "I think that person's best," and he receives the position. Somebody else may have another opinion. I may think that one person is better because I am better acquainted with him, but another may be better acquainted with the other candidate; in the end, the person designated is often not the one I had initially preferred. We all try to reach a concensus. Before the Party and the government, I merely outline my views, ideas, and opinions. There could be nothing further from one-man rule.

DYMALLY: Who will succeed you?

CASTRO: The Second Secretary of the Party would surely take over immediately, because he is the elected candidate of the Party, the Central Committee, and the Politburo. I think there should always be a Second and a Third Secretary, if possible, so there will be continuity. Of course, these are Party decisions, not made arbitrarily. Men are picked for their prestige, administrative record, and proven capability. Possibly the fact that there is a central cadre of officials prevents us from recognizing the potential capability of others. However, as the former die or retire, the latter must develop: this is a law of organizations that I have long experienced in practice. Governments which lose their leaders will quickly find replacements, who within a few days will be able to do the job perfectly well. For example, the Nicaraguan Revolution was started by Carlos Fonseca; when he died, others came forth to continue the struggle for victory.

I firmly believe in collective leadership—I don't think that history is made by individuals or personalities. I am well aware of what my role has been, and I realize that at a given moment it has been a very important role, because the ideas of one person can have a very great impact. To be successful, an idea must not be just the idle musings of an individual who thinks in a particular way; there must be millions of people who think the same way, and the idea expressed must encompass and reflect the collective hopes and dreams of society as a whole.

When I publish an interview of this kind, my views are passed on to the entire world. But I don't tell you journalists one thing and the Central Committee (or my people) something else. Not everything that was discussed with the U.S. delegation was released for publication, out of courtesy to your country, but everything I say to anyone can be published. There's not a single thing that I have said in diplomatic or trade negotiations that couldn't be released for public consumption.

We have millions of thinking people who are aware of current realities. At first, we were just a few, but those who replace us will be individuals of merit among many people with like merits. The authority we have is historical; the authority others will wield will be granted by established governmental and political institutions. It will be the Party which gives my successor his authority.

ELLIOT: Do you still embrace the view: "Men die, but the Party is immortal"?

CASTRO: That phrase is mine and it is still true. I have a philosophy about the relative value of individuals and the positions they hold. I remember what Martí said (one of the things I like most among his many marvelous ideas) which I have adopted as my own: "All the glory in the world can fit into a kernel of corn." If a leader thinks he is eternal or irreplaceable amidst all the honors and tributes, he fails to realize that all that is needed is for a few years to pass and nobody will even remember him. Yes, he may be mentioned every so often on an anniversary, and his accomplishments will be listed, such as they are, but he himself is gone. I have seen this often in the 26 years of the Revolution; I have seen leaders come and go, some dead, others replaced. Mao Tse-Tung was a god while alive; those who replaced him criticized him strongly. Ho Chi Minh was a great figure who will be long remembered, just as was Lenin. But others continued the work of Ho Chi Minh and obtained the victory he could not attain. It is the memory of men who forget themselves to serve a cause that lives on—and that cause itself.

In the future there will be people who are better prepared than we for our tasks, perhaps people not as experienced in one sense, but people with more education and training. Our country went through a most difficult stage when the economists, intellectuals, professionals, engineers, and doctors mostly left the country. The Revolution has replaced these people with thousands of new technicians who are better trained than their predecessors. Those who come after me will undoubtedly have their problems—we all have them—but they will also have the personnel and the economic resources that we couldn't even dream of when we started.

That is all I have to say about my role. I have never had any desire to resign. If you magnify the importance of what you are doing, you may feel that the world will be rocked by your departure. But if you don't give it much thought, but simply let matters take their course, someone else will eventually come forward. That is as it should be.

ELLIOT: Cuba is heavily dependent on the Soviet Union. Is such a proprietary relationship really in your country's best interests?

CASTRO: The United States is 90 miles away; the Soviet Union is 5000 miles distant. The United States is governed by an unequal pricing structure which it has imposed through the world economic system on the underdeveloped countries' products. But because your foreign debts are managed through private banks, your government often disclaims responsibility for the economic havoc your policies have caused in Latin America. If you discuss an economic problem with a socialist country, the government there can actually make a decision; it can extend a grace period, reduce interest rates, or even delay a debt for 10-20 years, without interest. That's what we're advocating for Latin America. These issues are raised and discussed and solved by governments; there's no need to involve 500 bankers. When we cancelled the Nicaraguan debt for the sugar mill construction, the decision was made by the Cuban state, not by a private bank; a bank couldn't do it. The Cuban state assumed the debt; it knows what resources it has, and it made the decision for reasons other than profit.

It's easier to discuss our economic problems with socialist countries, because it is not a system based on the ruthless egotism of capitalism. Things have gone very well for us, because our relations are based on revolutionary doctrines and ideas; capitalists seemingly have no doctrine save that of winning or losing money on a deal, selling high and buying low. But we have the possibility of discussing real issues and then reaching satisfactory agreements with socialist countries. Some countries have more resources—they can give more credits, and supply greater quantities of a given product. We consider specific situations. We trade with Vietnam at world market prices; our relations with Vietnam and Mongolia are different from those with the more developed nations. Similarly, China pays for our products at world market levels, which, of course, are now very low.

The Soviet Union is the most developed socialist country, the one with the most resources: then come countries like East Germany and Czechoslovakia. With all of them we have good relations and varying degrees of trade, depending on their needs and ours. There have never been political strings attached to our trade deals. Even during certain periods when international tensions were high, there was never any form of pressure put on us.

The fuel supplied by the Soviet Union has increased year by year, as have the supplies of other products. Even during the October Crisis, the flow of essential goods continued. Sometimes we have been critical of the Soviet Union, even publicly, but this has never led to any form of economic reprisals by socialist states against our country.

There was a period in the 1960s, I must admit, when we demonstrated a certain immaturity in international affairs, even a bit of extremism or arrogance. We felt we knew more about the world than other countries, and that we were more revolutionary than other socialist countries—we underestimated the value of experience. But we've matured, and they were very patient with us during that whole period. Of course, now we have the advantage of hindsight, and handle our affairs differently—more professionally, if you will. We can discuss anything. But we don't negotiate in public—no one does. The United States doesn't, but you still want us to engage in public debate with the socialist countries. However, when you have differences in policy with President Mitterand of France, these aren't often mentioned in your press, and if you have differences with Germany, England, or Japan, you have closed-door meetings to discuss them. They're your allies, after all, just as the socialist states are ours. Do not ask us to do what you would not do under similar circumstances.

Our slowly-acquired maturity has helped our relations with the socialist countries, which are now better than ever. The socialist countries respect Cuba—our intrinsic merit, revolutionary zeal, international awareness, and determination. We have been threatened, but we did not go down on our knees. We have neither surrendered nor sold out. The day that we do so is the day the Revolution disappears.

DYMALLY: How many political prisoners are there in Cuba?

CASTRO: Political prisoners, the old ones in Menoyo's category, the recalcitrant ones, once numbered in the thousands—they now amount to no more than a few hundred. Some from the Batista era are in prison still; nobody remembers them but us. I recently talked with the Catholic archbishops here to find some way of resolving the problem. Some of the prisoners were then released, most of whom will need visas so they can leave the country. Of the long-standing counterrevolutionary prisoners, there are perhaps 200, and there are a few hundred more who have served less time. I don't have the exact figures.

ELLIOT: Whenever this subject is raised, you always cite the same figures. Who are these individuals? What crimes, if any, did they commit? When will they be released?

CASTRO: There are some who have been in jail for a long time, the special group in which the United States has expressed interest (it doesn't seem interested in the handful of officials from the Batista era who still incarcerated).

They all have long sentences. There are also a few people who infiltrated the island at a later date, or carried out some other counterrevolutionary activities; but there aren't very many altogether. I have stated publicly that there was a period 20 years ago when there were some 15,000 prisoners incarcerated, during an era when the CIA was urging various counterrevolutionary organizations to subvert the government. Four or five people would get together and form a new group—the U.S. had prepared new invasion plans, and had infiltrated or funded armed bands in every province. There was a constant stream of mercenaries coming into the country, committing sabotage and murder, and doing everything possible to disrupt agriculture, industrial production, and transportation.

We released nearly all of those prisoners long before they had served their sentences. We did the same with the more than 1200 mercenaries who invaded our country and were captured; after they'd been held for a while, we said, "Pay us some compensation in food and medicine and we'll let you go." It was just a formula, because we didn't really need the supplies. We could have left them stewing in prison, I suppose, but to what end?—they were defeated men. So we sent a ship filled with "heroes" back to the U.S. Kennedy had already changed his policies by then.

Regarding the other category of prisoners, I told the bishops that everyone who comes from America brings a list handed them by the State Department containing the names of the counterrevolutionary prisoners most valued by the United States. The bishops replied: "Some of them have health problems." I told them: "We will investigate specific cases—if any of them have significant health problems, they will be released." Someone with eyesight problems or disabilities does not pose a threat to us, and we have no desire to seek vengeance against anybody. We are irritated when we see we're being pressured from outside—no one can interfere in our internal affairs. We have learned how to confront the most powerful country in the world, to defy its might and be prepared to suffer the consequences. But we do not harbor a spirit of revenge toward anyone.

Despite all the lies that your government and the mass media have printed about Cuba, there are many people in Latin America and in the Third World who trust and admire our country and its policies. Not in Europe, of course. Europe is very "sophisticated" and reads many right-wing newspapers. But we don't need much from Europe—or the United States—and I say that with the greatest of respect for the people living in those places. I believe that we have fulfilled our revolutionary role to the best of our abilities. History will take care of the rest!

ELLIOT: If you were suddenly given the opportunity to speak directly to the American people, what would you say?

CASTRO: The documents which frame your system of government express wonderful ideas—liberty, justice, the rights of men. But nowhere do you talk about the grinding poverty which infests the vast bulk of mankind, or the waste of talent, the lack of opportunity, the universal hunger, the miasma of disease, which permeate at least half of the people in the world, to a degree you freedom-loving people would find disturbing if you ever bothered to look beyond your television sets and two-car garages. The Cuban Revolution happened because you Norte Americanos were willing to use our island as a political and social playground while the vast majority of Cubans subsisted on beans and despair. The rights that I talk about are these: the right to an adequate diet for every man and his family, the right to as much education as the talents of each man allow, the right to a job and adequate income from that job, the right to decent health care for every man, the right to good housing, and the right to old-age benefits. If you ask the starving peasant in Ethiopia whether he wants the right to eat or the right to vote, which do you think he'll choose? I did not win the Cuban Revolution—the Cuban people won: my victories could not have happened, then or now, without their support.

We seek from you only your respect, as a co-equal partner in the community of nations. We do not ask for your dollars, we don't need your tourists, we're not begging you to pay our debts, and at this point we don't even need your grain. We are capable of taking care of our own affairs. All we ask is that you follow your own democratic precepts, and allow us to choose how we run this island of ours, under the system of government we believe is best suited to our problems and culture. We don't interfere in your affairs—please don't interfere in ours. If you adhere to just this one principle, you'll suddenly find that your "problems" in Latin America will have miraculously vanished overnight. Then we will all live together in peace. And when peace is guaranteed for all men, then the resources that are now being spent needlessly on useless weapons can be diverted to much more pressing concerns—like feeding and clothing and housing your brothers and sisters on this little planet of ours. And isn't that a nobler sentiment than any we've seen in a long, long time?

INDEX

JEFFREY M. ELLIOT & MERVYN M. DYMALLY

ABOUT THE AUTHORS

DR. JEFFREY M. ELLIOT is a professor of political science at North Caorlina Central University. A distinguished scholar, Dr. Elliot is a specialist in American politics and government, foreign policy and national security, civil rights and civil liberties, and political economy and Third World development. Dr. Elliot received his B.A. and M.A. from the University of Southern California, and his Ph.D. from Claremont Graduate School, as well as three honorary degrees. A prodigious writer, Dr. Elliot has authored or edited nearly 100 books and 550 articles, reviews, and interviews. His work has appeared in more than 250 publications, both in the United States and abroad, and he has been nominated for nearly 75 literary awards. His work spans such diverse fields as plitical science, history, sociology, eonomics, Black studies, criminal justice, literature, entertainment, the arts, sports, travel, science, and women's studies. An award-winning freelance journalist, Dr. Elliot has interviewed over 350 nationally- and internationally-known figures in American politics and world affairs. His interviews have been published, reprinted, excerpted, or quoted in numerous national and international publications, including *Newsweek, Time, Life, New Republic, U.S. News & World Report, Nation, New York Times, Boston Globe, Los Angeles Times, Village Voice,* and *Playboy,* among many others. He has served as editor or contributing editor to at least 15 magazines and journals, and has served on boards or as advisor to numerous civic and political organizations. A popular speaker on the lecture circuit, Dr. Elliot has delivered over 250 speeches and has appeared on more than 175 television and radio programs.

DR. MERVYN M. DYMALLY is president of Dymally International Group, Inc. He has served as a member of the United Staes House of Reprsentatives, Lieutenant Governor, State Senator, and Assemblyman (all from California). Dr. Dymally received his B.A. from California State University, Los Angeles, his M.A. from California State University, Sacramento, and his Ph.D. from U.S. International University, as well as nine honorary degrees. As a U.S. Congressman, he served on the Committee on Foreign Affairs, Subcommittee on Asian and Pacific Affairs, Subcommittee on International Operations (Chairman), Subcommittee on Africa (Chairman), Committee on Education, Subcommittee on Post Secondary Education, Committee on the District of Columbia, and Subcommittee on Judiciary and Education (Chairman), among others. he is the recipient of numerous honors and awards, including decorations from the Republic of Trinidad and Tobago, Central African Republic, Republic of Cote d'Ivoire, and Republic of Senegal. The founder of *The Community Democrat* and editor of *The Black Politician,* he is the author of several books and articles. He presently serves as honorary consul to the Republic of Benin, Visiting Lecturer at United States International University, President of the Center for the Study of the Harassment of African Americans, Chairman of the African Economic Agenda, Chairman of the Robert Smith Water Institute, Chairman of the California Water Caucus, Chairman of the California Political Institute, Chairman of the Caribbean Applied Research Institute, a member of the Democratic National Committee, and a member of the National Steering Committee, Clinton/Gore 1996 Campaign.

www.ingramcontent.com/pod-product-compliance
Lightning Source LLC
LaVergne TN
LVHW091309080426
835510LV00007B/440